John Gray is Professor of European Thought at the London School of Economics. His books include *Black Mass*, *Straw Dogs*, *Heresies* and *False Dawn*, which has been translated into thirteen languages.

Further praise for *Al Qaeda and What It Means to be Modern*:

'The most lucid advocate of the view that progress is an illusion.' Bryan Appleyard, *Sunday Times*

'John Gray interprets the true meaning of modern events and attitudes.' Iain Finlayson, *The Times*

'In this short, provocative book he expounds the notion that "al Qaeda is an essentially modern organisation", based not only upon Islam, but also upon the "West's ruling myth" of Utopian human perfectibility.' Anita Sethi, *Observer*

'A provocative take on what is often too quickly described as religious fundamentalism.' Pankaj Mishra, *New Statesman* (Books of the Year)

'John Gray, Professor of European Thought at the London School of Economics, and the natural heir to Isaiah Berlin, is the most clear-thinking of contemporary political philosophers . . . This new book is a characteristically unflinching assessment of the crisis in which we find ourselves post-September 11th.' John Banville, *Irish Times by the same author*

BLACK MASS:
Apocalyptic Religion and the Death of Utopia (Penguin)

HERESIES:
Against Progress and Other Illusions (Granta)

STRAW DOGS:
Thoughts on Humans and Other Animals (Granta)

FALSE DAWN:
The Delusions of Global Capitalism (Granta)

AL QAEDA
And What It Means to be Modern

JOHN GRAY

faber and faber

First published in 2003
by Faber and Faber Limited
3 Queen Square London WIN 3AU
Paperback edition first published in 2004
This paperback edition first published in 2007

Typeset by Faber and Faber Ltd
Printed in England by Mackays of Chatham plc,
Chatham, Kent

A CIP record for this book
is available from the British Library

ISBN 978–0–571–23842–2
ISBN 0–571–23842–4

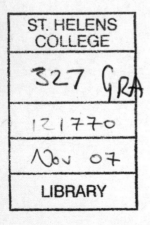

2 4 6 8 10 9 7 5 3 1

I dedicate this book to Mieko,
who made it possible.

Contents

Acknowledgements

In this short volume, I have developed a thought about Al Qaeda and what it means to be modern that I voiced in *Straw Dogs: Thoughts on Humans and Other Animals* (Granta Books, pp.174–6). The present book is somewhat different in style in that I have presented the argument more consecutively. Still, I hope that readers who are interested in specific topics can find and take what they want from the sections into which I have divided the book.

A number of people have helped me with this book. It could not have been completed without the guidance my editor at Faber, Neil Belton, gave me at every stage. Conversations with Adam Phillips were formative in my thinking about how the book might be written. Several people gave me valuable comments on draft versions. Among these, I would like to mention Bryan Appleyard, J. G. Ballard, Nick Butler, Robert Cooper, David Cornwell, Fred C. Ikle, Michael Lind, Shaun Riordan, G. W. Smith and George Walden. It goes without saying (but I say it anyway) that I alone am responsible for the book that has emerged.

John Gray

Introduction

The first edition of this book was written before the Bush administration launched its invasion of Iraq. It was already clear that the US would use military force to secure the overthrow of Saddam and that the result would be chaos on a large scale. It has come to be believed that the flaw in regime change was a failure to prepare for the aftermath of the attack, but in truth there were no policies that could have replaced Saddam's regime with one that was more legitimate. Regime change meant the break-up of the state and an intractable insurgency, followed by civil war as the country's rival communities fought to secure a share in its oil reserves. These are not dangers perceived by hindsight.[1] They were risks that were known at the time to the many Middle East scholars, diplomats and military and security advisers who cautioned against the war. Their advice was ignored, suppressed or distorted, with the results we see today.

The disaster that is unfolding in Iraq is a result of policies implemented on the basis of a utopian ideology rather than a realistic assessment of possibilities and consequences. Overthrowing a despot is futile if the result is to create a failed state: anarchy is as much a threat to human freedom as tyranny, often more so; and if the aim is to find and disable weapons of mass destruction, it will be harder to do so in conditions in which government has collapsed. Creating failed states is fairly easy; but no one knows much about how to rebuild them. The Bush administration knows nothing at all. Possessed by a messianic certainty that all that is needed for freedom to flourish is that tyranny be removed, it has created a situation whose outcome can only be a mix of anarchy and Islamist theocracy in much of what remains of Iraq.

Like most other states in the region, Iraq is a post-colonial construction whose popular legitimacy is precarious. A break-up of the state is now unavoidable, but a three-way partition of the country is highly unlikely. Such a solution would be acceptable neither to the Shia majority nor to the Sunnis who were in power under Saddam. Secession by the Kurds followed by decades of civil war is a more realistic prospect. There is the real possibility of a 'Shia crescent' emerging in the region in which communities belonging to that Islamic tradition seek power and resources hitherto possessed by Sunnis. As I wrote in the first edition of this book, 'Pursuing regime changes in the Middle East will effect a revolutionary unsettlement in the region not unlike that which was produced by President Woodrow Wilson's attempt to implement national self-determination in Central and Eastern Europe after the First World War' (p.94). This large-scale unravelling of regimes and power relations is now under way. It could be argued that the dissolution of the post-colonial states that make up most of the Middle East would be no bad thing, since it would enable the formation of others that might be more legitimate. Even if Islamist parties ruled them, as is more than likely, these new states might still be more accountable than authoritarian regimes left by departing imperialists. It is a reasonable argument, though it assumes that something like the European nation-state is feasible throughout the region – and worth the large cost in bloodshed and upheaval it would entail. Another, perhaps more realistic scenario is that the unravelling of post-colonial regimes that is now under way will leave a string of failed states in its wake with much of the region being effectively anarchic – a hugely expanded Lebanon. In any event it seems clear that, like Europe in the time of Woodrow Wilson, the Middle East is entering another era of war and revolution.

So much could be foreseen in the run-up to the American attack, but I did not write the first edition of this book in the fond belief that warning against the looming disaster would have any practical effect. American government was in the hands of radical ideologues, and like other such visionaries they believed that the condition of humanity could be transformed by the use of force. The neo-conservatives who were the pivotal force in the Bush administration at that time, and who are still the most influential element in it today, spurn the pursuit of stability in international relations. They aim for 'creative destruction' – the overthrow of existing regimes and the installation of western-style democracies. Part of the strategic rationale of the Iraq war was that it would enable American control of the country's oil reserves. Iraqi oil production would increase, the war would be self-financing, and regimes friendly to America would spring up all over the Middle East. None of this has come to pass, but the ambitions of the neo-conservatives are in no way diminished. Today they urge military action against Iran in order to secure regime change and the disablement of the country's nuclear programme.

Unlike most other countries in the region, Iran is a fairly cohesive state with an elected government. Undoubtedly there are oppositional forces, including some ethnic minorities, but the current regime's attempt to acquire nuclear capability is its most popular feature and gives it a degree of legitimacy it would not otherwise have. An American air campaign would increase this legitimacy and intensify the insurgency in Iraq, as Iranian-supported militias stepped up their attacks on US forces. It could also have a highly disruptive impact on the global economy, since the Iranian government has the capacity to block oil shipments in the Persian Gulf. At the same time it could not be relied upon to destroy all of the country's suspect nuclear facilities. Another American attempt at regime change would likely leave Iran in the hands of more extreme Islamist forces and still seeking nuclear capability, with incalculably destabilising consequences for the region. Even so, such an attempt – with or without the use of military force – is sure to be made.

Neo-conservative foreign policy is based on a utopian faith in creative destruction, not reason. The idea of creative destruction originated with Mikhail Bakunin, the nineteenth-century Russian anarchist who famously declared: 'The passion for destruction is a creative passion.'

The belief that human progress requires the destruction of existing institutions animated a long line of twentieth-century revolutionaries that includes Lenin, Trotsky and Mao. Its remoter origin is in the Jacobin faith in violence as a means of regenerating society, which produced the Great Terror in revolutionary France. Despite their position on the political spectrum, neo-conservatives belong in this Jacobin and Leninist tradition.[2]

Neo-conservative policies of regime change in the Middle East implement a right-wing version of modern utopian ideology. Many of the older generation of neo-conservatives began on the far left of American politics, where they were sustained by a fantasy of an imminent proletarian revolution that would sweep away capitalism and bourgeois democracy. Today some of the same people believe capitalism and bourgeois democracy are destined to replace all other systems. The neo-conservative theory of a 'global democratic revolution', which President Bush has cited as the basis of US policy in the Middle East, is a right-wing variant of Trotsky's theory of permanent revolution. It differs from Trotsky's in that it has the power of the world's most heavily armed state behind it. That will not spare it from a similar fate.

Trotsky's theory of permanent revolution was a sectarian variant of Leninism. Lenin believed that the new universal society that was emerging would only be established after great wars and savage revolutions involving the systematic use of terror. Trotsky shared this belief, and so do his neo-conservative disciples. There is a historical myth according to which the Bolshevik Revolution was hijacked by Stalin and would have turned out better had Trotsky been in charge. Given the cruelty that he demonstrated in the Russian civil war – when he introduced the practice of hostage-taking and crushed the revolt of workers and sailors in Kronstadt – the fate of Russia might well have been worse under a regime headed by Trotsky than it was under Stalin; but the upshot would have been no different. The Soviet regime practised oppression on a scale unprecedented in Russia for over seventy years, only to founder when confronted by the power of nationalism and religion in Poland, Afghanistan and the Baltic States. The global democratic revolution is a variant of Leninism that will not last anything like as long, but like the Soviet version it will founder after it has inflicted much needless suffering.

Neo-conservatives believed that the result of regime change in Iraq would be the spread of liberal democracy across the region and that the result would be an end to terrorism and the threat of WMD. In this they were doubly deluded. Democracy in Iraq and much of the Middle East means elective theocracy rather than anything resembling a liberal state, but liberal democratic regimes in the region would very likely also seek to acquire WMD. In the unlikely event that the current Iranian regime were to be replaced by something more like liberal democracy, the situation would not change. The same is true in Saudi Arabia, and in Iraq. In any realistically foreseeable future the Middle East will continue to be a dangerously unstable region with energy resources that the rest of the world urgently needs. Regimes of all types will seek to protect

themselves against attack from neighbours and from pre-
dation by great powers. If they can acquire WMD they will
do so. Creating a string of western-style democracies in
the region – if that were feasible – would not alter this fact.

Nor would the spread of liberal democracy curb terrorism. Many long-standing liberal democracies have produced powerful terrorist movements, and terrorism often
continues or increases when democracy replaces authori-
tarianism. The UK has struggled to contain terrorist activity by the IRA and its offshoots for decades, Italy was
subject for many years to major attacks by the Red
Brigades, Japan produced the Red Army Brigade and the
apocalyptic Aum cult that planted sarin gas on the Tokyo
Underground, Germany engendered the Baader–Meinhof
Gang while Spain still suffers from Basque terrorism
decades after its transition to democracy. The US has its
own problem of indigenous terrorism, as was seen in the
Oklahoma bombing. Again, despite its record as a stable
democracy, India has been subject to terrorism for many
years, while the Tamil Tigers developed in the context of a
functioning democratic system in Sri Lanka. On the other
hand, after a version of democracy was installed in Russia
it has suffered terrorism on a larger scale than anything
that existed in Soviet times, whereas authoritarian China
remains largely immune. There is no reliable correlation
between the spread of democracy and the decline of terrorism. If anything the link works the other way, with terrorism worsening when democracy is established in
contexts where there are deep-seated conflicts or
aggrieved national or religious minorities.

The belief that the ills of the Middle East can be cured by a conversion to western modernity ignores the central role of terror in modern western history. Saddam's regime was highly despotic and employed terror in a systematic way, but it was built on modern western models – the Stalinist Soviet Union and National Socialist Germany. The history of the twentieth century is largely one of the rise and fall of totalitarian regimes driven by radical western ideologies. Importing another of these ideologies into the fractured societies of the contemporary Middle East is a recipe for conflict and oppression on a larger scale than exists there already.

The destructive role of modern western ideology is already evident. To a degree that is not commonly acknowledged, radical Islam is a recent western construction. During the Cold War Islamist movements were funded and armed by the West as buffers against the Soviet Union. Al Qaeda was founded in the Soviet–Afghan conflict with western aid and support, and in many other contexts Islamist parties were used as instruments of western policy. Islamist ideologues define themselves in terms of enmity to the West, but they have often served as its proxies.[3] They also define themselves as anti-modern, but it should by now be evident that radical Islam is a by-product of late modern globalisation. In the case of Al Qaeda this is evident in the use of the technologies and types of organisation that go with the present phase of globalisation – encrypted Internet sites, offshore financial institutions and worldwide criminal networks, for example – and also in the nature of its ideological appeal. Al Qaeda gains strength from the collapse of traditional societies that is an integral feature of globalisation. The Utopia it envisions is not a return to the local cultures of the past but a universal civilisation in which such cultures will no longer exist. As Olivier Roy has put it: 'Fundamentalism is both a product and an agent of globalisation, because it acknowledges without nostalgia the loss of pristine cultures, and sees as positive the opportunity to build a universal religious identity, delinked from any specific culture.'[4]

The use of terror by radical Islamist groups has very little to do with traditional Islam and far more with the techniques of asymmetric warfare used by modern revolutionary movements. There is nothing peculiarly Islamic in suicide bombing. Until the Iraq war it was the Tamil Tigers, a Marxist–Leninist group that recruits mainly in Hindu communities, that had committed more suicide bombings than any other organisation, and the first suicide attack on Israeli soil was committed in 1972 by the Japanese Red Army. The use of suicide bombing by Hamas falls into the category of strategic terrorism analysed by Robert Pape in a notable recent study.[5] Cheap and highly effective, suicide bombing is the technique of choice for groups confronting overwhelming conventional military force.

Much suicide bombing can be analysed in these strategic terms, but Al Qaeda is more complex. While it has political objectives (such as the destruction of the Saudi regime), it also displays some of the features of contemporary cults. Al Qaeda has a strong appeal to deracinated Muslims in westernised societies: it provides meaning and purpose in lives that lack them and recreates an identity where one has been lost. The spectacular violence of Al Qaeda has been compared with that of the Assassins (or Hashashin), a twelfth-century heretical Ismaili sect that practised ritual assassination. It is better understood as a fusion of symbolic violence of the kind waged against capitalist institutions by groups such as the Baader–Meinhof Gang with overtly apocalyptic terror of the sort practised by the Japanese Aum cult.

The crucial point is that all these movements are modern. The Middle Ages were extremely violent, and gave birth to the revolutionary millenarian movements analysed by Norman Cohn as precursors of twentieth-century totalitarianism.[6] Yet the medieval world – Christian or Islamic – contained nothing like the revolutionary movements of the late modern period that aim to transform society by the use of force. In medieval times violence was accepted as a legitimate form of defence against tyrants. It was also often used against heretics, sometimes on a large scale. No one imagined that it could alter the human condition. The belief that a type of society better than any that has ever existed can be brought into being by the systematic use of violence belongs in our time, not that of our medieval ancestors. Like Jacobinism and Leninism, Nazism and Maoism, radical Islam is a uniquely modern pathology.

The belief persists that the modern period has witnessed a gradual movement towards societies based on reason and science. Much of the history of the last century was shaped by totalitarian movements that claimed to be based in science but were in fact fuelled by apocalyptic myths. In liberal societies we think we are immune to that type of irrationality. Radical ideologues may seize power in a backward country lacking modern democratic institutions, but not in a highly developed country. Dictatorships may be prone to utopian projects, but not liberal democracies. Free societies cannot be captured by revolutionary ideologues possessed by myths.

The rise and continuing power of neo-conservatism in the United States shows this liberal faith to be delusive. The last century was a time of myth-based politics and wars of faith – secular and religious. Al Qaeda and the War on Terror suggest that the present century is unlikely to be very different.

What Al Qaeda destroyed

The word 'humanity' is most repugnant; it expresses nothing
definite and only adds to the confusion of all the remaining
concepts a sort of piebald demi-god.
Alexander Herzen[1]

The suicide warriors who attacked Washington and New
York on September 11th, 2001, did more than kill thou-
sands of civilians and demolish the World Trade Center.
They destroyed the West's ruling myth.

Western societies are governed by the belief that
modernity is a single condition, everywhere the same and
always benign. As societies become more modern, so they
become more alike. At the same time they become better.
Being modern means realising *our* values – the values of
the Enlightenment, as we like to think of them.

No cliché is more stupefying than that which describes
Al Qaeda as a throwback to medieval times. It is a by-
product of globalisation. Like the worldwide drug cartels
and virtual business corporations that developed in the
Nineties, it evolved at a time when financial deregulation
had created vast pools of offshore wealth and organised
crime had gone global. Its most distinctive feature – pro-
jecting a privatised form of organised violence worldwide

– was impossible in the past. Equally, the belief that a new world can be hastened by spectacular acts of destruction is nowhere found in medieval times. Al Qaeda's closest precursors are the revolutionary anarchists of late nineteenth-century Europe.

Anyone who doubts that revolutionary terror is a modern invention has contrived to forget recent history. The Soviet Union was an attempt to embody the Enlightenment ideal of a world without power or conflict. In pursuit of this ideal it killed and enslaved tens of millions of human beings. Nazi Germany committed the worst act of genocide in history. It did so with the aim of breeding a new type of human being. No previous age harboured such projects. The gas chambers and the gulags are *modern*.

There are many ways of being modern, some of them monstrous. Yet the belief that there is only one way and that it is always good has deep roots. From the eighteenth century onwards, it came to be believed that the growth of scientific knowledge and the emancipation of mankind marched hand in hand. This Enlightenment faith – for it soon acquired the trappings of religion – was most clearly expressed in an exotic, sometimes grotesque but vastly and enduringly influential early nineteenth-century intellectual movement that called itself Positivism.

The Positivists believed that as societies came to be based on science they were bound to become more alike. Scientific knowledge would engender a universal morality in which the aim of society was as much production as possible. Through the use of technology, humanity would extend its power over the Earth's resources and overcome the worst forms of natural scarcity. Poverty and war could be abolished. Through the power given it by science, humanity would be able to create a new world.

There has always been disagreement about the nature of this new world. For Marx and Lenin, it would be a classless egalitarian anarchy, for Fukuyama and the neo-liberals a universal free market. These views of a future founded on science are very different; but that has in no way weakened the hold of the faith they express.

Through their deep influence on Marx, Positivist ideas inspired the disastrous Soviet experiment in central economic planning. When the Soviet system collapsed, they re-emerged in the cult of the free market. It came to be believed that only American-style 'democratic capitalism' is truly modern, and that it is destined to spread everywhere. As it does, a universal civilisation will come into being, and history will come to an end.

This may seem a fantastical creed, and so it is. What is more fantastic is that it is still widely believed. It shapes the programmes of mainstream political parties throughout the world. It guides the policies of agencies such as the International Monetary Fund. It animates the 'war on terror', in which Al Qaeda is viewed as a relic of the past.

This view is simply wrong. Like communism and Nazism, radical Islam is modern. Though it claims to be anti-western, it is shaped as much by western ideology as by Islamic traditions. Like Marxists and neo-liberals, radical Islamists see history as a prelude to a new world. All are convinced they can remake the human condition. If there is a uniquely modern myth, this is it.

3

In the new world as envisaged by Al Qaeda power and conflict have disappeared. This is a figment of the revolutionary imagination, not a prescription for a viable modern society; but in this the new world envisioned by Al Qaeda is no different from the fantasies projected by Marx and Bakunin, by Lenin and Mao, and by the neo-liberal evangelists who so recently announced the end of history. Like these modern western movements, Al Qaeda will run aground on abiding human needs.

The modern myth is that science enables humanity to take charge of its destiny; but 'humanity' is itself a myth, a dusty remnant of religious faith. In truth there are only humans, using the growing knowledge given them by science to pursue their conflicting ends.

Three modern projects

> Europe in 1914 had perhaps reached the limit of modernism . . .
> Every mind of any scope was a crossroads for all shades of opin-
> ion; every thinker was an international exposition of thought.
> There were works of the mind in which the wealth of contrasts
> and contradictory tendencies was like the insane displays of
> light in the capitals of those days . . . How much material wealth,
> how much labour and planning it took, how many centuries
> were ransacked, how many heterogeneous lives were combined,
> to make possible such a carnival, and to set it up as the supreme
> wisdom and the triumph of humanity!
>
> Paul Valery[1]

A hundred years ago, Europe viewed itself as the model for
the world. Backed by overwhelming economic and military power, its civilisation seemed superior to all others.
Most Europeans had no doubt that in the course of the
twentieth century European values would be accepted
everywhere.

In a sense, they were right. Soviet communism,
National Socialism and Islamic fundamentalism have all
been described as assaults on the West. In reality, each of
these three projects is best understood as an attempt to
realise a modern European ideal.

The catastrophe of the First World War jolted European

self-confidence, but it also created the conditions for the twentieth century's most ambitious attempt at modernisation on a European model. The Soviet experiment was made possible by a European civil war. Yet it was unequivocally a European project.

The Cold War is still sometimes called a conflict between East and West; but this is to forget the genuine conflict between Eastern Orthodoxy and western Christianity that long preceded it. If Russia has never been an unambiguously western country, one reason is that in religion it has always defined itself by opposition to the West. Far from being an enemy of 'the West', Soviet communism was one of many failed attempts to westernise Russia.

For many years western scholars sought to explain the Soviet system as a reversion to Muscovite traditions of tyranny and barbarism. The truth is nearer the opposite. Tsarist Russia had many flaws. There were many hideous pogroms; but mass killing with the aim of perfecting humanity was not among the Tsars' crimes. That began in Russia with Lenin, who rightly saw himself as standing in a tradition of revolutionary violence going back to the Jacobins.

The Soviet system undoubtedly made use of Russian traditions of despotic rule; but it was not born in an Orthodox monastery. It was an attempt – by no means the first, or the last – to implant a western regime in Russian soil. Russia did not become a western country after the Soviet collapse. It reverted to its historic ambiguity towards the West – an ambivalence that was deepened by

6

the ruinous results of another attempt to reconstruct it on a western model.

Soviet communism was conceived in the heart of western civilisation. It could not have originated in any other milieu. Marxism is only a radical version of the Enlightenment belief in progress – itself a mutation of Christian hopes.[2]

By no means all Enlightenment thinkers warmed to the idea of progress. Even Voltaire – the supreme *philosophe* – did not subscribe to it consistently.[3] Yet Marx was at one with the main current of Enlightenment thought in affirming that the growth of knowledge enables mankind to shape a future better than anything it has known in the past.

As everyone knows, Marx turned Hegel's philosophy upside down. Where Hegel asserted that history was a succession of evolving concepts, Marx claimed it was changes in society's material basis that governed the development of ideas. What is less often noted is that Marx and Hegel's view of history could only have arisen in a Judaeo-Christian culture.

Hegel and Marx followed Judaism and Christianity in seeing history as a moral drama whose last act is salvation. In other cultures this view is unknown. For the Greeks and Romans as for the Indians and the Chinese, history has no overarching meaning. It is a series of cycles, no different from those we find in the natural world.

Marxism is an Enlightenment philosophy based on a Judaeo-Christian view of history. In other words, it is a prototypically western doctrine. That is how it was received in Russia, where Bolshevism became one more westernising project. Ever since Peter the Great, a section of Russian opinion had seen the only salvation for their country in becoming a fully European country. Lenin's dictatorship was only another in a series of attempts to modernise Russia on a European model.

From the start the Bolsheviks aimed to copy what they took to be the most advanced features of European life. Rapid industrialisation was imperative. Peasant life had to be eradicated and farming reorganised on a factory model. Mass production – organised on the basis of the American engineer F. W. Taylor's studies of time and motion in the work place, which Lenin greatly admired – was the only route to prosperity. Following Marx, the Bolsheviks believed that human emancipation required industrialisation. Industry was an expression of human power over Nature. By turning the natural world over to industrial uses, humanity could satisfy its needs. At the same time it could imprint a human meaning on the Earth.

As faithful disciples of Marx, the Bolsheviks aimed to humanise Nature. They began by collectivising agriculture. The result was to destroy Russia's capacity to feed itself. Millions of peasants died by starvation and in camps. Large parts of Russia turned into dustbowls. The terror and misery of the Soviet period left indelible marks in the Russian soil. Nature was humanised.

The roots of the Soviet system were in the Enlightenment's most utopian dreams. Lenin never gave up the belief that, after a period of revolutionary terror, the state would be abolished. Trotsky defended the taking and killing of hostages as a necessary stage on the way to a world in which every human being would have the gifts of Michelangelo and Shakespeare. A vast amount of blood was spilt pursuing these sickly dreams.

The result of the attempt to realise the Bolshevik utopia was a totalitarian regime.[4] This was not a deformation of Marx's original vision. Despite innumerable claims to the contrary, this was the only result it could have had in practice. Marx's conception of communism presupposes that the chief source of human conflict is the division of society into classes. Once that has been overcome, state power is unnecessary.

In reality the roots of human conflict are more deeply tangled. Class divisions are only one of the causes of conflict, and rarely the most important. Ethnic and religious differences, the scarcity of natural resources and the collision of rival values are permanent sources of division. Such conflicts cannot be overcome, only moderated. The checks and balances of traditional forms of government are ways of coping with this fact.

The attempt to abolish the state results in unlimited government. Lenin laid the foundations for Stalin's regime. In turn, Lenin's dictatorship was inherent in Marx's ideal of communism. Totalitarianism follows wherever the goal of a world without conflict or power is consistently pursued.

If Soviet totalitarianism was a result of flaws in Enlightenment thought, so was its collapse. It was not economic failure that destroyed the Soviet state. The trigger

9

came from forces that – according to the view of the modern world accepted by Marx and, later, by neo-liberals – ought no longer to exist.

No doubt historical accident played a role. Ronald Reagan's Star Wars may have been more an exercise in disinformation than a realistic programme of national defence; but they convinced a segment of the Soviet élite that the system had to change to survive. Mikhail Gorbachev emerged in response to a perception that the Soviet regime had become stagnant and corrupt; but the only real result of his reforms was to reveal its complete lack of legitimacy. Uniquely, the Soviet state fell apart without significant violence on the part either of the rulers or the ruled.

Standing behind the weakness of the Soviet regime was the undiminished strength of nationalism and religion. Poland became the first post-totalitarian country partly through the strength of the Church. Afghanistan was able to resist Soviet invasion because of the power of Islamic fundamentalism – at that time supported by the West.

The Soviet experiment failed, and at colossal human cost. Even so, it was repeated in many other countries. During the Maoist period, the Soviet system was the model for economic development in China. When China deviated from the Soviet model – as it did, in some respects, during the Cultural Revolution – it was in order to realise a more authentic form of socialism. The result was even worse than in Russia – enormous loss of human life and liberty, together with massive environmental degradation. Only when the Marxist inheritance was rejected in the 1980s did China begin to follow a path of its own.

In both its scale and in its goal of bringing into being a new, socialist humanity, Soviet terror was uniquely modern. The same is true of the Nazi genocides.

Nazism was a mix of bad and mad ideas. Theosophists and occultists jostled with anti-Semitic Christians and votaries of new state cults for the worship of Norse gods; proponents of a degraded version of Herder's Romantic nationalism marched at the side of propagandists for 'scientific racism'. To essay any definitive view of such a hotchpotch is hazardous. Yet it is clear that the Nazis were far from being unambiguously hostile to the modern world, or to the Enlightenment.

There was never any doubt in Hitler's mind that Nazism was a modern project. An ardent admirer of Henry Ford and American techniques of mass production, the Nazi leader saw technology as a means of enhancing human power. Science enabled humanity – or some portion of it – to take charge of evolution. A superior species would be bred from the best human types. As for the rest, they would be exterminated or enslaved.

If the threat posed by the Nazis was not widely understood, it was partly because they were so modern. The Edwardians who ruled Britain in the Thirties came from a world of hansom cabs and country houses decorated with the paintings of Reynolds and Gainsborough. They exercised power through parliamentary institutions and a highly stratified social structure. The Nazis came from a world of autobahns and heavy industry. They used mass rallies to destroy parliamentary institutions and mass media as a means of reshaping society. If they had artistic precursors, they were in avant-garde movements such as Expressionism and Futurism.

When it was understood, Nazi modernism was often admired. Hitler's view of the world had some elements in common with that of sections of Europe's progressive intelligentsia. Left-leaning scientists such as J. D. Bernal and Julian Huxley toyed with the idea that science could be used to create a higher species. G. B. Shaw and H. G. Wells had a strong interest in positive eugenics. Many socialists (including a number of early Fabians) were fascinated by Nietzsche's ideas. Anti-Semitism was commonplace, with writers such as Hilaire Belloc and Wyndham Lewis writing at length on 'the Jewish problem'. It is only in retrospect that Nazi ideas appear anomalous. At the time, they were only an extreme version of what many people believed.

Nazism is often seen as an attack on western values.[5] In fact, like Soviet Communism, it embodied some of the most powerful western traditions. The Nazis despised Enlightenment ideals of toleration, personal freedom and human equality. Even so, they shared the Enlightenment's most hubristic hopes. Like Marx, they believed that the power of technology could be used to transform the human condition.

The Nazis viewed themselves as revolutionaries on a par with the Jacobins and the Bolsheviks. In Arthur Koestler's wartime novel *Arrival and Departure*, a philosophising Nazi diplomat – a type that was common

12

at the time – declares that Nazism is more internationalist than the French Revolution or Soviet Communism:

Don't you realise that what we are doing is a real revolution and more internationalist in its effects than the storming of the Bastille or the Winter Palace in Petrograd? . . . Close your eyes. Imagine Europe up to the Urals as an empty space on the map. There are only fields of energy; hydro-power, magnetic ores, coal-seams under the earth, oil-wells . . . Wipe out those ridiculous winding boundaries, the Chinese walls which cut across our fields of energy; scrap or transfer industries which were heedlessly built in the wrong places; liquidate the surplus population in areas where they are not required; shift the population of certain districts, if necessary of entire nations, to the spaces where they are wanted and to the type of production for which they are racially best fitted; wipe out any disturbing lines of force which might super-impose themselves on your net, that is, the influence of the churches, of overseas capital, of any philosophy, religion, ethical or aesthetical system of the past . . .

The Nazis repudiated the past and embraced modern technology as an instrument of human power – including the power to commit genocide on a hitherto unprecedented scale:

We have embarked on something – something grandiose and gigantic beyond imagination. There are no more impossibilities for man now. For the first time we are attacking the biological structure of the race. We have started to breed a new species of *homo sapiens*. We are weeding out its streaks of bad heredity. We have practically finished the task of exterminating or sterilising the gipsies in Europe; the liquidation of the Jews will be completed in a year or two . . . We are the first to make use of the hypodermic syringe, the lancet and the sterilising apparatus in our revolution.[6]

Nazi success attracted conservative supporters in many European countries, not least Germany itself, but the Nazis never sought the restoration of a traditional social order. As Herman Von Rauschning, a Prussian conservative and member of Hitler's inner circle until he was forced to flee Germany with a price on his head, put it: 'National Socialism is an unquestionably genuine revolutionary movement in the sense of a final achievement on a vaster scale of the "mass rising" dreamed of by Anarchists and Communists.'[7]

In many European countries, notably Vichy France, Nazism found support among those who saw in it a way of forestalling social revolution. As they soon found out, they were mistaken. Like communism, Nazism aimed to revolutionise society and remake humanity.

It is a mistake to think that opponents of liberal values are enemies of the Enlightenment. Embracing science and technology, Soviet Communism and Nazism were each animated by ambitions that derive from the Enlightenment. At the same time they were thoroughly anti-liberal.

Could anything like Nazism be repeated? Only a few years ago, a nearly universal consensus proclaimed that globalisation was forcing a movement to the centre ground of politics. In fact, as could be foreseen, it has fuelled extremism.

In Europe at the start of the twenty-first century, parties of the far right are not survivals from an earlier era. They are certainly atavistic in their racism and anti-Semitism, but they are embarked on an unmistakably modernist experiment. The European far right is not so much a rerun of fascism as an attempt to modernise it. Like the Nazis, it is developing a version of modernity that encompasses some of Europe's darkest traditions.

There are some differences between Europe in the interwar period and today. Then mass parties dominated political life; now political parties are in decline. When large numbers of people are mobilised it is in single-issue groups like Greenpeace and amorphous networks such as the anti-capitalist movement. In the interwar period, democracy was enfeebled in much of Europe; now it is entrenched. Then there was severe economic crisis. Now – for the time being – Europe is muddling through.

These differences account for the far right's changed strategies. The Nazis overthrew democracy. Today the far right is exploiting it. The Nazis mobilised the unemployed and those threatened by unemployment. The new far right is targeting workers whose incomes and position in society are threatened by the shift of manufacturing industries and – increasingly – of service industries to developing countries. Following the conventional wisdom of the time, the Nazis favoured corporatist economic policies. Today, while drawing support from groups threatened by globalisation, the far right embraces it. Aside from Le Pen's National Front, Europe's new far right has adopted a conventional neo-liberal economic programme.

It is no accident that over the past decade Europe has witnessed a resurgence of the far right. As in the interwar period, the radical right understands the fragility of liberal societies better than most of their defenders. The far right has moved from the margins of politics to the centre by understanding that globalisation has losers, even in the richest countries, and linking their fortunes with immigration and the remoteness of European institutions. Parties of the far right are in national government in a number of European countries, such as Austria and Italy. In others, such as Denmark and Holland, they are shaping the agenda of politics.

Europe may be the prototype of a post-modern state, in which national governments co-exist with powerful supra-national institutions.[8] If so, this is far from being an irreversible development. European institutions cannot supplant historic national identities, but they can erode them. Such weakened national cultures are ideal breeding grounds for the far right.

The European Union represents itself as an alternative model of modern development with the potential to rival the United States. Yet the project of turning the Union into a single economy is an attempt to imitate America's continent-wide free market. Aside from compromising the distinctive virtues of European capitalism, this is a project whose failure is pre-ordained by European history. America's labour mobility is made possible by a strong national culture. With its long settled territories and fractious nationalities, Europe can never have mobility on an American scale. Nor is such mobility clearly desirable. Yet it is a prerequisite if a single currency is not to lead to explosive economic imbalances.

There is nothing natural about the nation-state. It is a distinctively modern construction. In time, other forms of political order may supersede it. But for the present the nation-state marks the upper limit of democracy – on which the legitimacy of government today depends. In effect, the European attempt to move beyond the nation-state is an attempt to move beyond democracy. Some such movement may be inevitable, but it gives the far right a dangerous appeal.

At the same time that Europe is embarked on the experiment of going beyond the nation-state, building nation-states remains the basis of development throughout the world. In some ways this is unfortunate. As I shall argue when I discuss failed states in Section 7, it is often impossible to replicate the European nation-state. Even where it has proved feasible, it is a costly enterprise.

The most successful experiment in modernising on a European model occurred in Turkey. The Ataturkist regime has lasted longer than the Soviet Union. In terms of its support in society it has incomparably greater legitimacy. Yet it is coming under growing pressure from Islamist movements. The future of the European model in Turkey is an open question. Outside Europe, some of the most successful experiments in modernisation have been in countries that have grafted new technology onto their indigenous cultures. While the attempt to emulate European models led to disaster in Russia, Asian countries have made far more selective borrowings from the West. Even so, they have not been able to avoid European modernity entirely.

The paradigm case of indigenous modernisation is Japan.[9] Contrary to liberal and Marxist theories of history, industrialisation in Japan did not entail the break-up of a feudal social order. It developed on the basis of social institutions inherited from the feudal age. Today Japan is a mature industrial society fully comparable with Britain or Germany. It has not accepted western values, and shows no signs of doing so. Nevertheless, it has been compelled to make extensive borrowings from western sources, some of them unfortunate.

After the arrival of Commodore Perry in 1853, Japan had no alternative to making itself over as a European nation-state if it was not to become a western colony like China and India. Modernisation involved turning a folk religion – Shinto – into a state cult, not unlike Protestant Christianity in post-Reformation Europe. Japan became the first Asian country to defeat a European power at the Battle of Tsushima in 1905, when the Japanese navy destroyed the Russian imperial fleet; but it was a victory that led on to a period of militaristic nationalism. In order to resist the European powers, Japan was forced to emulate them.

If China and India follow Japan in seeking to modernise on the basis of their indigenous traditions rather than western models, they too will still find themselves imitating some western practices. Not all of these borrowings will be desirable.

India is cited by western commentators for its success in developing new industries, such as those involved in software production. The success is real enough, but it has come from ignoring western ideas. Except in one or two regions, India never embraced Marxism; and it has stubbornly resisted the more recent neo-liberal cult. As a result of its relative immunity to western ideologies, India avoided the catastrophes that befell China during the Maoist period and Russia in the neo-liberal Nineties; but it has been forced to adopt some aspects of European modernity.

The movement to reform Hinduism that developed in the late nineteenth and early twentieth centuries emulated British examples. The Hindu youth movement was modelled on the Boy Scouts. Hinduism itself was redefined, so that an unfathomably complex body of beliefs and practices could – like Shinto – become more like a western religion. In an effort to resist western influences, western ideas and types of organisation were imported into India.

China faces similar dilemmas. The Chinese government has consistently spurned western economic advice. In this it has acted very sensibly, as is shown by the fact that the West now applauds its wisdom. In order to attract such western admiration, however, China needs to be strong enough to resist western power.

China's rulers are bent on turning the country into a strong modern state; but in so doing they are walking a European path. As we know it today, the French nation is an artefact of military conscription and the school system. Using these institutions, the Napoleonic state created a national culture that had not existed before, wiping out a wide diversity of languages and traditions on the way. Today, the Chinese state is doing the same in Tibet. In using the power of the state to forge a national culture, China is following a European precedent.

Countries that seek to modernise on the basis of their

own cultural traditions rather than western models are wise. In resisting western power, however, they cannot avoid becoming in some ways like the European proto- types of the modern state. No country can escape the imperatives of the modern world that Europe created.

A third modern movement claims to reject the modern world. Radical Islam sees itself as an enemy of modern val- ues. Many of its opponents have accepted this view. As one commentator wrote, distilling a mass of confusion into a single formula: 'September 11th was an attack on modernity by Islamic fascists.'[10] In fact, radical Islam is like fascism chiefly in being unequivocally modern.

Movements with some affinities to radical Islam began to appear in Europe at the time of the break-up of medieval order. Reformation Christians such as Jan Huss in early fifteenth-century Bohemia rejected the authority of the Church in order to return to the purity of the biblical message. Around the same time, Thomas Muntzer in Germany was preaching a millenarian type of Christian- ity that soon came to be associated with visions of a new society. For several centuries, despite periods of persecu- tion, a network of adepts – the Brethren of the Free Spirit – was active in many parts of Europe. This millenarian movement rejected not only the authority of the Church but that of morality as well.[11]

Medieval societies suffered many savage conflicts, but they were founded on a belief in authority. Early modern millenarian movements rejected established authority. In this they are precursors of radical Islam; but they did not imagine that a wholly new world could be brought into being by acts of terror. Truer precursors of radical Islam can be found in the late nineteenth-century European revolutionary movements that turned to propaganda by deed.

Revolutionary terrorism developed in late Tsarist Russia against a background of rapid change. Cities were expanding; literacy was growing; population growth was rapid; a new class of unemployed intellectuals was emerging. Russia had all the marks of a fast-modernising society. The dislocated students who took to terror as a political weapon did not hark back to a mythical past – as the millenarian cults did in Bohemia and Germany several centuries earlier. Modern men and women, they looked instead to a mythical future.

Their view of it was extremely hazy. They were more interested in the act of destruction itself than in its supposed benefits. The father of Russian anarchism, Mikhail Bakunin, summed up this attitude in a celebrated dictum: 'The passion for destruction is also a creative passion.' For those who acted on this slogan, terrorism was a triumph of the will.

There are differences between Al Qaeda and European revolutionary anarchism. Late nineteenth-century anarchists targeted public officials, not civilian populations. They used terror sparingly. In contrast, Al Qaeda aims to inflict mass civilian casualties. Even so, it has more in common with these modern European revolutionaries than it does with anything in medieval times. If Osama bin Laden has a precursor, it is the nineteenth-century Russian terrorist Sergei Nechaev who, when asked which members of the House of Romanov were to be killed, answered: 'All of them.'

In his novel *The Secret Agent*, Joseph Conrad gives a vivid picture of this kind of revolutionary nihilism. Conrad has the First Secretary to the Russian Embassy in London observe that if terrorism is to be effective it must be an attack on society's most cherished beliefs: 'The sacrosanct fetish of today is science.' Accordingly, the Russian diplomat instructs his agent provocateur to blow up the Royal Observatory at Greenwich. Attacking a building devoted to the science of astronomy would be 'an act of destructive ferocity so absurd as to be incomprehensible, inexplicable, almost unthinkable'. For that very reason it would be highly effective: 'Madness alone is truly terrifying, inasmuch as you cannot placate it by threats, persuasion or bribes.'[12]

In Conrad's time, the sacrosanct science was physics. Today it is economics. Al Qaeda destroyed a building devoted to trade, not one dedicated to the study of the stars. The strategy is the same – to remake the world by spectacular acts of terror.

No one did more in laying the intellectual foundations of radical Islam than the Egyptian thinker Sayyid Qutb. Born in 1906 in a small village, he moved to Cairo to live with an uncle, where he obtained his first job as an inspector in the Ministry of Education. His true vocation was as a writer. The several volumes of Quranic commentary he produced in prison are still widely read among Islamic militants. Influenced by Abdul Ala Maududi (1903–79), a Pakistani ideologue who first used the concept of *jihad* or

22

holy war in an explicitly political context, Qutb became the chief thinker of the Muslim Brotherhood. He was executed by Nasser in 1966.

The central theme of Qutb's writings is the spiritual emptiness of modern western societies. Like many Americans, Qutb saw the US as the paradigm of modern society. He lived in America for several years. He failed to notice that it is one of the most religious societies in the world.

Starting with de Tocqueville, many perceptive visitors have noted the intense religiosity of America. According to the standard, social-scientific theory of advanced, knowledge-based societies, America should be following Europe in becoming steadily more secular; but there is not the slightest evidence for any such trend. Quite to the contrary, America's peculiar religiosity is becoming ever more strikingly pronounced. It has by far the most powerful fundamentalist movement of any advanced country. In no otherwise comparable land do politicians regularly invoke the name of Jesus. Nowhere else are there movements to expel Darwinism from public schools. In truth, the US is a less secular regime than Turkey.

To see America as a godless society is extremely curious, but it is of a piece with Qutb's monocular view of the world. It did not occur to him that if America is modern, so is fundamentalism. Very likely the thought could not have occurred to him. If it had, he would have understood that he was also modern.

In any event, it was the freedom of American life that most aroused Qutb's hatred. Joining a church social club, he was horrified by the overt sexuality that was displayed as 'arms circled arms, lips met lips, chests met chests' while members danced to the tune of 'Baby, It's Cold Outside' under the benign eye of the pastor. He condemned the attention Americans gave to their garden lawns as an expression of a lack of community spirit. He attacked jazz as 'a type of music invented by Blacks to please their primitive tendencies and desire for noise'.[13]

Qutb's writings are filled with horror of the West, but he borrowed many of his ideas from western sources. He was especially indebted to European anarchism. The idea of a revolutionary vanguard dedicated to bringing into being a world without rulers or ruled has no precedents in Islamic thought. It is a clear borrowing from European radical ideology. As Malise Ruthven has written: 'The message of revolutionary anarchism implicit in the phrase that "every system that permits some people to rule over others be abolished" owes more to radical European ideas going back to the Jacobins than to classical or traditional ideas about Islamic governance. Similarly the revolutionary vanguard Qutb advocates does not have an Islamic pedigree . . . The vanguard is a concept imported from Europe, through a lineage that also stretches back to the Jacobins, through the Bolsheviks and latter-day Marxist guerrillas such as the Baader–Meinhof gang'.[14]

Qutb's ideas about revolutionary struggle were of recent European vintage. So was his approach to the Quran, which he regarded in ultra-modern fashion not as a repository of literal truth but as a work of art. For Qutb, faith was an expression of subjectivity, a personal commitment

24

made by an act of will. As Binder has put it: Qutb 'seems to have adopted the post-Kantian aesthetic of liberal individualism that was the legacy of European romanticism to the cultural elite of the colonial world'.[15]

The intellectual roots of radical Islam are in the European Counter-Enlightenment.[16] In this current of thought, which began to take shape in the late eighteenth and early nineteenth centuries, the rational scepticism of Enlightenment thinkers such as David Hume led to a rejection of reason itself. J. G. Hamman rejected rational inquiry in favour of religious revelation. Kierkegaard defended religious faith in terms of subjective experience. J. G. Herder rejected the Enlightenment ideal of a universal civilisation, believing there are many cultures, each in some ways unique. Later in the nineteenth century, thinkers such as Fichte and Nietzsche glorified will over reason.

It is the fact that radical Islam rejects reason that shows it is a modern movement. The medieval world may have been unified by faith, but it did not scorn reason. Its view of the world came from a fusion of Greek rationalism with Judaeo-Christian theism. In the medieval scheme of things, Nature was believed to be rational.

The Romantic belief that the world can be reshaped by an act of will is as much a part of the modern world as the Enlightenment ideal of a universal civilisation based on reason. The one arose as a reaction against the other. Both are myths.

In the nineteenth century, Romanticism was a German protest against the French claim to embody universal civilisation. In the early twenty-first century, Romantic ideas have returned as part of the resistance to American universalism. Al Qaeda sees itself as an alternative to the modern world, but the ideas on which it draws are quintessentially modern. As Karl Kraus said of psycho-analysis: radical Islam is a symptom of the disease of which it pretends to be the cure.

3

The original modernisers

The distribution of the forces of tradition,
entrenched over thousands of years of history, cannot be
grasped in any quantifiable way.
Leszek Kolakowski[1]

The history of ideas obeys a law of irony. Ideas have consequences; but rarely those their authors expect or desire, and never only those. Quite often they are the opposite.

The Positivists are the original prophets of modernity. Through their influence on Marx, they stand behind the twentieth century's communist regimes. At the same time, by their formative impact on economics, they inspired the utopian social engineers who constructed the global free market in the aftermath of the collapse of communist central planning.

The Positivist catechism had three main tenets. First, history is driven by the power of science; growing knowledge and new technology are the ultimate determinants of change in human society. Second, science will enable natural scarcity to be overcome; once that has been achieved, the immemorial evils of poverty and war will be banished forever. Third, progress in science and progress in ethics and politics go together; as scientific knowledge advances and becomes more systematically organised, human values will increasingly converge.

This Positivist creed animated Marx's ideal of communism. It informed the 'theories of modernisation' that were developed after the Second World War. It guides the architects of the global free market today.

The founder of Positivism was Count Henri de Saint-Simon (1760–1825).[2] Saint-Simon used to instruct his valet to waken him each morning with the words 'Remember, monsieur le comte, that you have great things to do.' Perhaps as a result, he had an eventful life. At the age of seventeen he was commissioned into the army and served with the French forces in the American War of Independence. Later in his military career he was taken prisoner and interned in Jamaica, after which he conceived the first of many grandiose schemes – a plan for a canal linking the Atlantic and the Pacific through Lake Nicaragua, which he unsuccessfully submitted to the Viceroy of Mexico. He amassed a fortune during the French Revolution by buying up houses vacated by noblemen who had emigrated or been guillotined. For a time he seems to have served as an agent of the British Foreign Office.

In later years Saint-Simon fell on hard times. Falsely accused of instigating an assassination, he spent some years in a private hospital for the insane. The daily reminders of his greatness given him by his manservant did not enable Saint-Simon to achieve the success to which he aspired. In his last years it was only the support that he received from his devoted servant that kept him from starvation.

Saint-Simon was an adventurer. He was also the first modern socialist. He analysed society into distinct classes, each with a different relationship to the means of production, and attacked market capitalism as anarchic, wasteful and chronically unstable. Saint-Simon's critique of capitalism was hugely influential. But more influential still was his vision of the future of humanity, which at the close of the twentieth century re-emerged in the utopian project of a universal free market.

According to Saint-Simon, actually existing societies are chaotic and divided; but that is because they have not absorbed the findings of science. Progress in society is a by-product of progress in science. As knowledge advances, so does humanity.

Every society must pass through a series of definite stages. Each must move from a religious view of the world to a metaphysical outlook, and from that to the positive – or scientific – stage. In each of these three stages, human knowledge becomes more definite and – a vitally important point for the Positivists – more systematically organised. In the end, when all societies have passed through these stages, ethics will become a science, no less objective in its results than physics or chemistry. At this point, the moral and political conflicts of the past will disappear.

Where there is no conflict there is no need for power. As Marx put it in a phrase he borrowed from Saint-Simon, the government of men will be replaced by the administration of things. Marx knew little of the work of Comte, whom he read only in the late 1860s and then dismissed; but the influence on him of Saint-Simon was profound. With the growth of knowledge and the continuing expansion of production, Saint-Simon believed, the state will wither away. Marx followed Saint-Simon in this conviction, which became the core of his conception of communism.

The Positivists did not aim merely to revolutionise society. Their aim was to found a new religion. Saint-Simon believed the 'positive doctrine' would become the basis for a new 'church' when all scientists united to form a permanent 'clergy'.[3] He envisaged an assembly of 'the twenty-one elect of humanity' to be called the Council of Newton. Newton's idea of universal gravitation was 'the basis of the new scientific system'. It should also be the basis of 'the new religious system'.[4] In Saint-Simon's new religion, however, it was not gravity that replaced the Deity. That place was filled by humanity. Saint-Simon's last work was the *Nouveau Christianisme* (1825) – a new version of Christianity in which the human species became the Supreme Being.

The practical transformation of Positivism into a religion began not long after Saint-Simon's death, when – as one historian of the movement puts it – 'The Saint-Simonians transformed themselves into a religious cult'.[5] Soon the Positivist cult acquired all the paraphernalia of the Church – hymns, altars, priests in their vestments and its own calendar, with the months named after Archimedes, Gutenberg, Descartes and other rationalist saints.

Auguste Comte (1798–1857), the most influential of the Positivist savants, completed the transformation of Positivism into a religion. The son of a local government official, Comte began his career by entering the Ecole

Polytechnique in Paris in 1814 on the basis of a brilliant performance in the national entrance examination. It has been said of the young *polytechniciens* of this period that they believed that 'one could create a religion in the same way as one learned at the Ecole to build a bridge'.[6] Comte's approach to the design of a new religion was decidedly more emotional than rational, but like his peers in the Ecole Polytechnique he had an almost unlimited faith in the power of social engineering.

Comte began by ridiculing the cult that had grown up around Saint-Simon. Once Saint-Simon's protégé, he broke with him acrimoniously; thereafter he acknowledged no intellectual debt to the older man. Yet he took up Saint-Simon's idea that Positivism should become a religion and promoted it with a passion that verged on madness.

The development of Comte's system of ideas cannot be understood outside the context of his private life. Like his relationship with Saint-Simon, Comte's first marriage in 1822 ended in acrimony. His wife had nursed him through the first of many mental collapses, keeping him at home when a psychiatrist had declared him incurably deranged, and submitting to a bizarre Christian marriage ceremony (demanded by Comte's mother, who objected to their common-law union) in which Comte – by then suffering from paranoia – signed himself Brutus Napoleon Comte.

In an eerie rerun of Saint-Simon's career, Comte's mental instability recurred throughout his life. It was displayed in his relationship with Mme Clothilde de Vaux, a gifted and attractive married woman abandoned by her husband.

Comte's affair with Clothilde was never consummated. She died tragically after a struggle with illness (probably tuberculosis). Comte was once again driven to the brink of insanity.

The motif of all Comte's later work and the inspiration of his new religion is well summarised by Manuel: 'After Clothilde's death Comte's whole life became devoted to a religious worship of her image.'[7] In a number of works written after her death, Comte scandalised his rationalist disciples by declaring love to be the moving force of humanity. They were further dismayed when he went on to nominate Clothilde as the Virgin Mother of the Church of Humanity and ordained that her grave be a place of pilgrimage.

There was method in Comte's madness. Taking the Catholic Church as his model, he devised a minute system of daily observances for followers of the new religion. In his *Système de Politique Positive* (1852–4), he laid down that the pious Positivist should pray three times a day for a total of two hours, once to each of his household goddesses, his mother, wife and daughter. He was to cross himself by tapping his head with his finger three times at the points where – according to the science of phrenology – the impulses of benevolence, order and progress were situated. There were nine Positivist sacraments, beginning with Presentation, an equivalent to baptism in which the infant was to be given two patron saints, and ending with the Sacrament of Incorporation. When he died, the good Positivist's remains would be deposited in the sacred wood surrounding each Positivist temple. At that point his memory would be incorporated into the Supreme Being. These observances were to be regulated by the Grand Pontiff of Humanity, who was to reside in Paris. In his will, Comte appointed thirteen executors, who were to preserve his lodgings as the permanent headquarters of the Religion of Humanity.

Comte specified the duties and organisation of the Positivist clergy as follows:

During the seven years which elapse before he is full priest, every vicar must teach all the seven encyclopaedic sciences, and exercise his powers of preaching. After that he becomes a true priest . . . Every philosophical presbytery has seven priests and three vicars. Their residences may be changed by the High Priest . . . The number of these priestly colleges will be two thousand for the whole Western world. This gives a functionary for every six thousand inhabitants, or one hundred thousand for the whole earth.

With unwitting humour, Comte wrote: 'The rate may appear too low; but it is really adequate for all the services required.'[8]

The Positivists approached the construction of the new religion with an obsessive concern for detail. New forms of clothing were invented. Waistcoats were designed with the buttons on the back, so that they could be put on and taken off only with the assistance of other people. The aim was to promote altruism and cooperation. Sadly, the result was to provoke raids from the police, who – taking Saint-Simon's talk of 'the rehabilitation of the flesh' literally – suspected his disciples of taking part in orgies.

The Positivist religion – 'Catholicism minus Christianity',

as T. H. Huxley called it – was eminently ridiculous. It was also extremely influential. Temples of Humanity sprang up not only in Paris but also in London, where a chapel was founded in Lamb's Conduit Street, and in Liverpool. The Positivist Church was notably successful in Latin America. In Brazil, where Comte's slogan 'Order and Progress' is part of the national flag, there are active Positivist temples to this day. In France, Comtean ideas of rule by a technocratic élite had a lasting influence in the Ecole Polytechnique. Through his deep impact on John Stuart Mill, with whom he maintained a long correspondence, Comte was instrumental in identifying liberalism with secular humanism – or, as Mill and Comte termed it, the Religion of Humanity.[9]

With all its absurdities, the Religion of Humanity is the prototype of the secular religions of the twentieth century. Marxism and neo-liberalism embody its central tenet: with the growth of scientific knowledge, mankind can rid itself of the immemorial evils of human life – war, tyranny and scarcity.

Saint-Simon and Comte inherited this Enlightenment faith from the Marquis de Condorcet (1743–94). Condorcet was the author of a celebrated essay on the progress of the human mind in which he asserted the perfectibility of human nature. Will not the growth of knowledge demonstrate, he asks, that 'the moral goodness of man is susceptible of indefinite improvement, and that nature links together truth, happiness and virtue by an indissoluble chain?'[10] Condorcet died in prison after being arrested by the revolutionary government of Robespierre.

Saint-Simon and Condorcet may well have met; but in any case Saint-Simon, and later Comte, imbibed from Condorcet the most fundamental beliefs of the Religion of Humanity: The advance of science is not an accident; it is a result of the nature of the human mind, which is inherently progressive. Allied with mankind's innate goodness, science can transform the human condition.

With Condorcet, Saint-Simon and Comte believed that the progress that humanity has achieved in government and society is an inevitable result of the progress of the human mind. History is only the development of human intelligence, itself inevitable, in which the truths discovered by science are used to transform society. There is a law of progress in human affairs, from which the future of the species can be predicted. Saint-Simon wrote: '. . . the progress of the human mind has reached the point where the most important reasoning on politics can and must be deduced directly from the knowledge acquired in the high sciences and the physical sciences. It is my aim to imprint a positive character on politics.'[11]

Saint-Simon and Comte looked forward to a 'positive' politics, in which science would be used to emancipate mankind. That is not to say they were liberals. Like Marx, they believed the advance of science made liberal individualism redundant. Unlike Marx, they viewed the Middle Ages with sympathy. As a result, they sought out alliances with conservative thinkers.

Comte asserted that history oscillated between 'critical' periods such as his own time and 'organic' periods. To be sure, he never imagined that society could return to the past. As an Enlightenment thinker, Comte was committed to the idea that humanity could someday live better than it had ever done in the past; but as an admirer of organic societies he incorporated elements from the past into his vision of the future. Partly for this reason, Positivist thought has had a recurring appeal for the European right, surfacing in the Thirties on the intellectual fringes of fascism.

Both Saint-Simon and Comte were attracted by the ideas of Joseph de Maistre. An ultra-orthodox Catholic, de Maistre was a life-long enemy of the Enlightenment. It may be hard to see what the leading savants of Positivism could have in common with such a relentlessly reactionary thinker. Yet, Saint-Simon surmised, the future of mankind may lie in a fusion of de Maistre and Voltaire – a thought to which I return in the last section of this book.

The chief appeal of Positivism to the right came from the conviction of Saint-Simon and Comte that a science of society must be based solidly on the truths of physiology. Saint Simon always emphasised that physiology is central and fundamental in any 'science of man'. Comte aimed to develop what he called a 'social physics', a physiologically based social science with which – he declared – 'the philosophical system of the moderns will be in fact complete.'[12] In that it gave a patina of intellectual authority to a belief in basically different human types, the idea that social science should be grounded in physiology had obvious attractions to the European Right.

It would be absurd to hold Saint-Simon and Comte responsible for developments of their ideas of which they could know nothing; but there is a clear line of thought linking pseudo-science such as phrenology with the political ideas of the far right in Europe in the twentieth century. Comte's use of phrenology has already been noted. Later in the nineteenth century, phrenology was to feature in the 'criminal anthropology' developed by the Italian jurist Cesare Lombroso (1835–1909). Positivist ideas shaped Lombroso's thinking in a number of ways. In Lombroso's view, there is an innate disposition to criminal behaviour, and it can be detected by the study of physiology and physiognomy. Favouring a judicial system in which experts played a leading role, he proposed using the techniques of 'anthropometry'. These involved measuring facial and cranial features, along with height and other physical characteristics, as a means of identifying criminals and 'criminal types'. Lombroso's anthropometric methods were used in the Italian judicial system and in many other countries right up to the Second World War.

Phrenology was also used to develop racial theories. In the 1860s, the founder of the British Anthropological Institute, John Beddoe, developed an 'Index of Nigrescence' based on cranial characteristics, which he used to support the claim that the Irish were 'Africanoid'. In the twentieth century, 'craniometric' techniques were used by the Nazis to distinguish 'Aryans' from 'non-Aryans'.

On Left and Right, the appeal of Positivism came from its claim to possess the authority of science. Nearly always, the appeal to science went with the rejection of liberalism. Yet this protean doctrine re-surfaced at the end of the twentieth century among those who aimed to make a narrow version of liberal values universal.

If Positivism is the chief source of the twentieth century's most powerful secular religions it is partly through its impact on the social sciences. For Positivists, modernity is the transformation of the world by the use of scientific knowledge. For Comte, the science in question was sociology – of a highly speculative sort. For ideologues of the free market, it is economics – a no less speculative discipline. But whatever the science, its conclusions are supposed to apply everywhere.

In Positivist methodology, social science is no different from natural science. The model for both is mathematics. Nothing can be known unless it can be quantified. Applying this view, Comte invented sociology – a term he coined; but the idea that mathematics is the ideal form of human knowledge proved most powerful in economics, where it helped spawn the idea of a global free market.

Without realising it – for few of them know anything of the history of thought, least of all in their own subject – the majority of economists have inherited their way of thinking from the Positivists. Working their way into the discipline via Logical Positivism, Saint-Simonian and Comtean ideas have become the standard methodology of economics.

Saint-Simon and Comte envisaged a unified science in which all of human knowledge would be reduced to a single set of laws. For Saint-Simon, the evolution of the human mind would not be complete until the whole of knowledge was shown to obey a single law. He wrote that, in the twelfth and last stage in the development of the

38

human intelligence: 'The general system of our knowledge will be reorganised on the basis of the belief that the universe is ruled by a single immutable law. All the systems of application, such as the systems of religion, politics, morals and civil law, will be placed in harmony with the new system of knowledge.'[13] In much the same spirit, Comte wrote: '. . . the first characteristic of the positive philosophy is that it regards all phenomena as subjected to invariable natural laws. Our business is . . . to pursue an accurate discovery of these laws, with a view to reducing them to the smallest possible number.'[14]

The project of a unified science means that the social sciences are no different in their methods from the natural sciences. Both seek to discover natural laws. The only genuine knowledge is that which comes from scientific inquiry; and every science – including the social sciences – aspires to the generality and certainty of the laws of mathematics. For, as Comte declared, 'mathematics must . . . hold the first place in the hierarchy of the sciences'.[15]

The idea that the study of society should form part of a single unified science came into economics from the Vienna Circle – a group of scientists and philosophers that met in Vienna from 1907 onwards. After the appointment to a professorship at the University of Vienna of the philosopher Moritz Schlick in 1922, the Vienna Circle achieved considerable success as the disseminator of Logical Positivism.

The Vienna Circle sprang partly from the philosophy of Ernst Mach (1838–1916), a physicist and expert in ballistics who was hugely influential in Vienna at the turn of the century. Like Comte, Mach held that religion and meta-physics belonged in a primitive phase of the mind. Science alone gave knowledge of the world. In Mach's view, scientific knowledge was a construction from human sensations. A synthesis of Comte and Mach, the Vienna Circle viewed science as a combination of the necessary truths of logic and mathematics with data gleaned from the senses.

The core of Logical Positivism was the development of a scientific worldview. Going further than Saint-Simon and Comte, the Logical Positivists declared that only the verifiable propositions of science have meaning: strictly speaking, religion, metaphysics and morality are nonsense. In philosophy, in the writings of the early Wittgenstein, this doctrine reappeared as a mystical theory of the limits of language. In social science, it boosted the aspirations of economics to be a rigorous discipline on a par with physics and mathematics.

With the rise of Nazism, the Vienna Circle was scattered, many of its members fleeing to the United States. As a clearly defined movement in philosophy, Logical Positivism ceased to exist by the 1940s. Yet it had a formative impact on economics, shaping the views of Milton Friedman and many others.

None of the classical economists believed that mathematics should be the model for social science. For Adam Smith and Adam Ferguson, economics was grounded in history. It was bound up inextricably with the rise and decline of nations and the struggle for power between different social groups. For Smith and Ferguson, economic life can only be understood by examining these historical developments. In a different way, the same is true of Marx. Since the rise of Positivism in the social sciences this tradition has practically disappeared.

The decoupling of economics from history has led to a pervasive unrealism in the discipline. The classical economists knew that the laws of the market are only distillations from human behaviour. As such, they have the limitations of all types of historical knowledge. History demonstrates a good deal of regularity in human behaviour. It also shows enough variety to make the search for universal laws a vain enterprise. It is doubtful if the various forms of social studies contain a single law on a par with those of the physical sciences. Yet in recent times the 'laws of economics' have been invoked to support the idea that one style of behaviour – the 'free market' variety found intermittently over the past few centuries in a handful of countries – should be the model for economic life everywhere.

Economic theory cannot show that the free market is the best type of economic system. The idea that free markets are the most efficient mode of economic life is one of the intellectual pillars of the campaign for a global free market; but there are many ways of defining efficiency, none of them value-free. For the Positivists, the efficiency of an economy was measured in terms of its productivity. Certainly the free market is highly productive. But as Saint-Simon and Comte understood very well, that does not mean it is humanly fulfilling.

The idea that the free market should be universal makes

sense only if you accept a certain philosophy of history. Under the impact of Logical Positivism, economics has developed into a thoroughly unhistorical discipline. At the same time, it has imbibed a philosophy of history that derives from Saint-Simon and Comte.

According to Positivism, science is the motor of historical change. New technology drives out inefficient modes of production and engenders new forms of social life. This process is at work throughout history. Its end-point is a world unified by a single economic system. The ultimate result of scientific knowledge is a universal civilisation, governed by a secular, 'terrestrial' morality.

For Saint-Simon and Comte, technology meant railways and canals. For Lenin it meant electricity. For neo-liberals it means the Internet. The message is the same. Technology – the practical application of scientific knowledge – produces a convergence in values. This is the central modern myth, which the Positivists propagated and everyone today accepts as fact.

In some ways, the Positivists were wiser than their twentieth-century disciples The idea that maximal productivity is the goal of economic life is one of the most pervasive – and pernicious – inheritances of Positivism; but it is an idea to which Saint-Simon and Comte did not hold consistently. They knew that humans are not just economic animals. As the growth of knowledge accelerates, they believed, the maintenance of social ties becomes ever more necessary.

At their best, Saint-Simon and Comte were not dogmatists. They knew that human life is extremely complicated –

so much so that what is good in one society may be bad in another. Like Voltaire, they understood that in the real world of human history the best regime is not everywhere the same. In practice, if not in theory, the Positivists accepted that there is more than one way of being modern.

The architects of the global free market lack this wise political relativism. For them, only irrationality stands in the way of the best regime becoming universal. Nevertheless, the world they imagine they are building is unmistakably that envisaged by the Positivists. In a famous passage at the close of his *General Theory* (1936), Keynes wrote:

... the ideas of economists and political philosophers, both when they are right and when they are wrong, are more powerful than is commonly believed. Indeed, the world is ruled by little else. Practical men, who believe themselves to be exempt from any intellectual influences, are usually the slaves of some defunct economist. Madmen in authority, who hear voices in the air, are distilling the frenzy of some academic scribbler of a few years back.[16]

Keynes was writing at a time when public policy was governed by outdated economic theories. Today it is ruled by a defunct religion. To link exotic figures such as Saint-Simon and Comte with the vapid bureaucrats of the International Monetary Fund may seem fanciful, but the idea of modernisation to which the IMF adheres is a Positivist inheritance. The social engineers who labour to install free markets in every last corner of the globe see themselves as scientific rationalists, but they are actually disciples of a forgotten cult.

4

A very short history
of the global free market

Another belated, confused and imprecise word is the
current political-sociological term of 'modernisation'. If it
means anything, it is a confused and feeble substitute word
for something like Americanisation.

John Lukacs[1]

At the end of the Cold War, Francis Fukuyama declared
that the US embodied the final form of human government. Twelve years later, from a leftist standpoint only
seemingly opposed to Fukuyama's neo-conservatism,
Michael Hardt proclaimed an American empire. In the
event, the new millennium anticipated by these apocalyptic American ideologues lasted little more than a
decade.[2]

In the longer sweep of history the Cold War was an
anomaly. In strategic terms, it reflected a bipolar world. In
intellectual terms, it was a family quarrel between western
ideologies. Its end signalled the failure of the twentieth
century's most ambitious westernising project. Given an
event of this magnitude, the result could only be another
era of geopolitical conflict.

Russia was fated to endure another attempt to remake it
on a western model. The collapse of communism coincid-

ed with the high point of the free market. If they had possessed a smattering of history, the social engineers who tried to install a version of American capitalism in Russia would have known that their task was impossible.

In the last decades of the nineteenth century Russia had one of the most dynamic capitalist economies in the world; but it was a hybrid of state-dominated industries and wild entrepreneurship, not a western-style free market.[3] A realistic programme of economic transition in post-communist Russia would have aimed to nurture some such hybrid, not to implant an idealised version of American capitalism.

A large part of the responsibility for the fiasco of market reform in Russia lies with the failure of western-led financial institutions to understand the importance of the state. Western financial institutions viewed the state – or what was left of it in Russia – as an obstacle to economic reconstruction. It was a stance that ensured the failure of the planned transition.

Applying policies of 'shock therapy' that had produced mixed results in the very different conditions of Latin America, the IMF demanded a rapid roll-back of state power. Price controls were scrapped. Many of the country's assets were hastily privatised, with nothing being done to develop a law of property and contract. In Soviet times, something between a third and a half of the economy was given over to the military-industrial complex. Dismantling this sector required massive state intervention. Instead the state was dismantled. The end-result of western-sponsored market reform in Russia was a period in which the economy was ruled by the power of organised crime.[4]

The debacle of the free market in Russia was another failed attempt at modernisation, whose practical effects were akin to those of agricultural collectivisation. True, millions did not die of starvation; but fertility and life expectancy fell precipitously, leading to a population collapse on a scale unprecedented in a developed country. Most people survived by living on the produce of smallholdings. Having set out to become an industrial power, the country fell back on subsistence agriculture. Once again, it seemed, Russia had failed to catch up with the West, but in fact Russia was on the way to surpassing it. The transition from central planning to a western-style free market failed, but the mafia-based economy that emerged from the ruins of the Soviet state has evolved into a hypermodern type of capitalism.

Because of its origins in crime, Russian capitalism is well adapted to thrive in a time when the fastest growing sectors of advanced western economies are illegal industries such as drugs, prostitution and cyber-fraud. While Western economies have come close to bankrupting themselves in the pursuit of the fantasy of a 'weightless', knowledge-based economy, Russia is poised to become rich by exploiting looming shortages of natural resources. Under the aegis of Vladimir Putin's subtle authoritarian regime, Russia is now in the vanguard of economic development.[5]

Elsewhere in the world, market fundamentalism has led to a new type of reverse development, in which advanced countries revert to more primitive modes of economic life.

This is the pattern in Argentina. A century ago, it was among the world's most highly developed countries. Today it is an impoverished chaos.

It is customary to date Argentine economic decline from the time that the populist dictator Peron took power in 1946. In fact, the economy grew at a stronger rate in the Peronist decade than it did later. For much of the period after control of its economy passed to the IMF, Argentina's economy actually shrank. Nor is it true that Argentina's collapse resulted from its failure to reform its economy. The Argentine disaster would have been more complete if it had fully implemented IMF policies. As it does everywhere, the IMF demanded fiscal austerity. Argentina complied by making severe budgetary cuts. The result – known in advance by most economists, though not by those in the IMF – was that the economy, already contracting, shrank still further. As Joseph Stiglitz has put it: 'Not surprisingly, the cuts exacerbated the downturn; had they been as ruthless as the IMF had wanted, the economic collapse would have been even faster.'[6]

In the aftermath of the IMF's experiment, Argentina is a showcase example of reverse development. The large middle class it once had is ruined. A highly advanced market economy has been replaced by a barter economy. A quarter or more of the population is unemployed. Hunger is widespread. Crimes such as kidnapping and armed robbery are commonplace. With the economy and society in a state of collapse, a further change of regime must be on the cards.

To reduce a modern state to the level of a Third World regime in less than a decade is a remarkable achievement, but IMF policies in Argentina were no different from those it has imposed in other countries. As it blunders and bungles its way across the world, the IMF's goals do not change. However different the problems, the solutions are always the same. The IMF aims to install one sort of capitalism everywhere. Inevitably, given the diverse histories and circumstances of the countries that have been subject to its policies, this goal has proved elusive.

The global free market is not the result of competition between different economic systems. Like the free market that was created in England in the mid-nineteenth century, it was established and maintained by political power. Unlike its English precursor, the global free market lacks checks and balances. Insulated from any kind of political accountability, it is much too brittle to last for long.

The end of the Cold War left the US in a position of unchallenged power. The sense of national decline that had dogged the US throughout much of the Eighties was forgotten. The spectacular boom in American financial assets that raged throughout much of the Nineties boosted the long-held American belief that the US is a chosen nation. It was easy for American policy-makers to believe that the American free market would spread everywhere. Using their control of the IMF and the World Bank, they sought to accelerate this process. It seems not to have occurred to them that the US would become a casualty of the regime they were constructing.

The global free market is the offspring of a marriage of Positivist economics with the American sense of universal mission. It was only in the last decades of the twentieth century that Positivist thought came to be associated with the defence of free markets. Earlier in American history, the influence of Positivist thought worked against the idea of the free market. The impact of Comtean ideas can be seen clearly in Herbert Croly's book, *The Promise of American Life* (1909).[7] In this manifesto of American Progressive thinking, Croly – a political theorist and journalist who together with Walter Lippmann founded the *New Republic* – argued that America must renounce its individualism and develop strong national government. Within the Progressive movement, the rejection of individualism has another source in Hegel's thought. Many Progressives joined Woodrow Wilson in admiring Bismarck's Prussia as a model for the modern state.

In the last decades of the twentieth century, American social science was deeply informed by the Comtean idea – transmitted to the US by the Vienna Circle – that mathematics is the model for every branch of scientific knowledge. In economics, this methodology found expression in the idea of efficiency. American economists followed the Positivists in thinking that productivity is the best measure of economic efficiency, but lacked their understanding that productivity alone does not make a humanly acceptable economy.

Other intellectual traditions were important in spreading the idea that the free market is the only rational economic system. Latter-day disciples of Adam Smith's classical economists and votaries of the Austrian School were missionaries for the same idea. Despite these other influences, it was the Positivist doctrine that economic efficiency is measurable in terms of productivity that gave the free market the authority of science.

As in Europe, so in America, science – in this case, the nominal science of economics – was used to propagate a new religion.[8] The claims of economics as a science were linked with an indigenous American myth. The American free market was elevated to the status of a universal economic system.

For the Founders, America was an experiment. The experiment might fail. In any case it required a complicated set of initial conditions that did not exist anywhere else. There was nothing to suggest that the American form of government could be made universal. Despite this, many Americans have long believed that their country has a universal mission. It is not an uncommon conviction. The British in the nineteenth century, the French in the eighteenth, the Spanish and the Portuguese in the seventeenth and sixteenth – all imagined themselves to be precursors of a universal civilisation. There is nothing exceptional about American exceptionalism.

For much of the nineteenth century, the American sense of having a unique destiny was embodied in protectionism. In the last decade of the twentieth century the Soviet collapse left the US a mega-power at a time when the prestige of the free market – political and academic – had never been higher. Only then did the US embark on the project of constructing a global free market.

One of the props of this project was the belief that the US had discovered the secret of uninterrupted prosperity. Through a combination of deregulation in financial markets, free trade and new technology, it was claimed, the US had abolished the business cycle and achieved a permanent increase in American productivity.[9]

Joseph Schumpeter – a truly great economist who was much quoted during the Nineties – had written of the gale of creative destruction that goes with capitalism's high productivity. Theorists of the New Paradigm believed that a New Economy had been born, in which Schumpeter's gale had become a gentle breeze.

As always, the reality was more familiar. America's *fin-de-siècle* boom was a classic bubble. The only novelty was its size. Larger than any in history, it was pumped up by very large quantities of cheap credit and an influx of foreign capital.

Part of the attraction of investing in the American economy during this period came from the notion that it had achieved a large and permanent increase in productivity. The evidence for this is highly questionable. American economic statistics employ a method known as hedonic accounting, which allows for changes in the quality of goods. The effect of using this method of accounting is to inflate American productivity. Nearly all of the increase claimed by New Era publicists may be an artefact of this accounting convention. As a British observer has put it: 'The effect (of hedonic accounting) is that reported US GDP growth overstates the real growth of US output by half of one percent a year. This accounting difference is equivalent to the main part of the productivity miracle that still enthuses believers in the new economy.'[10]

Another factor ensured that America's boom would be

short-lived. The very fact that it was believed that the business cycle was no longer in operation ensured that it would return with a vengeance. When investors believe that central banks have engineered an end to the boom-bust cycle a major bust cannot be far off. Financial markets are not self-regulating systems. As Hyman Minsky and George Soros have shown,[11] they are inherently unstable; never more so than when they are generally believed to be stable.

Foreign capital was seduced by exceptionally creative accounting practices and Soviet-style productivity statistics into investing in an economic miracle that very likely never existed. This was always a highly unstable situation. With the decline in trust in US accounting standards that followed the collapse of Enron, one of the chief sources of the 'American economic miracle' – the influx of foreign capital – came into question.

In a curiously predictable reversal of fortune, the US is now at the mercy of the regime of free capital flows it imposed throughout the world in the Nineties. The instability that showed itself in the so-called Asian crisis and in the Russian debt default has reached the epicentre of the global free market. The result will be a global economic dislocation with geopolitical ramifications.

There have been several signs of growing strain. The Asian crisis that erupted in 1997 was interpreted in western countries as a symptom of the peculiar vices of Asian capitalism. Actually, it was triggered by a speculative attack on the Thai currency in July of that year. As could be seen at the time, it was an early warning of a systemic financial crisis.[12]

So long as they are confined to the peripheries of the global market, the destabilising effects of unfettered capital movements can be safely ignored. They can even be quite profitable – as when American stock and bond markets benefited from their safe haven status during the Asian and Russian crises. Yet it is in the logic of global *laissez-faire* that financial crisis will eventually impact in the heartlands of the system.

A global financial crisis very nearly resulted when Long-Term Capital Management, a hugely leveraged hedge fund founded by a pair of Nobel Prize-winning economists in which a number of central banks were heavily invested, collapsed after the Russian government defaulted on its foreign debt in August 1998. In the event, the threat was neutralised; but the fragility of the global financial system had been exposed.

By doing all they could to project the free market throughout the world, American policy-makers ensured that its inherent instabilities became global in scope. In times of boom, synchronous movements in world markets enhance prosperity. In the same fashion, they worsen the damage done in a time of bust. The conjunction of market globalisation with the aftershocks of the American bubble has created a particularly perilous situation. The world economy has come to rely on high levels of American consumption to maintain demand. If American consumers cut back their spending severely, the result could be a global economic dislocation on a scale larger than any since the Thirties.

America's options in dealing with the aftermath of the

bubble are narrow. With their retirement plans destroyed by the collapse of the stock market, Americans need to rebuild their finances.[13] If there are further stock market falls, or if the bubble that has been encouraged to develop in the real estate market bursts, they may become serious savers again. In that case, consumption will fall and recession – almost certainly global in scope – will follow.

In order to avert this outcome, the Federal Reserve Bank has embarked on a radical Keynesian programme of restarting the economy; but whereas the policies advocated by Keynes in the 1930s were designed to drag the economy out of depression, Mr Greenspan's hyper-Keynesian experiment is an attempt to prolong an unsustainable boom. Having failed to puncture the 'irrational exuberance' he detected on Wall Street in a speech made in December 1996, the Chairman of the Federal Reserve Bank gave it another lease on life.[14]

Other countries have had monetary and fiscal orthodoxy thrust upon them by the IMF. The US is under no such constraint. It has never been bound by the Washington consensus. Well before September 11th, short-term interest rates were reduced to low levels. Because it led to them being lowered still further, the overall economic impact of the terrorist attacks was stimulatory. If – as seems likely – low interest rates do not work, other more unorthodox measures will be tried. The power of the Federal Reserve Bank should not be underestimated. Even so, it is not the final arbiter of the American economy

The US may be the last superpower, but it cannot dictate the behaviour of global markets. In the course of history's largest stock market bubble it has become the world's greatest debtor. American living standards now depend on inflows of foreign capital continuing at the extremely high rates of the recent past. If they do not, the dollar will fall and financial crisis will follow.

Most American commentators insist that the deflation that has plagued Japan for a decade cannot occur in the US. Their confidence does not appear to be shared by the Federal Reserve Bank, which is known to have studied the Japanese experience closely. In fact, if deflation were to come to the US it would be much more damaging than it has been in Japan.

Japan remains the only true economic superpower. It is the world's greatest creditor; its households are among the world's greatest savers. The US is the world's largest debtor; its household savings are still negligible. If deflation comes to the US it will be even harder to control than it has been in Japan. That is one reason why the American monetary authorities will resort to any ruse to stave it off. In the US, the threat of deflation is sure to produce inflation – a development that will further reduce the willingness of foreigners to hold American assets.

The American model has some distinctive virtues, such as its openness to immigrants and its high level of entrepreneurship; but the appeal it had during the Nineties has ebbed away. Few other countries envy US levels of economic inequality, or its level of mass incarceration.[15]

Japanese citizens enjoy a level of personal security equal or superior to that of the Swiss – despite the fact that in Japan the prison population is proportionately around a twentieth of that in the US. In Europe, French and German workers work somewhere between eight and twelve weeks less each year than their American counterparts – though their incomes are growing while those of the American working majority have long been stagnant or falling. Few Asians or Europeans take seriously the claims of an economic model whose much-touted productivity gains have proved to be largely fictitious, in which major companies have become little more than highly leveraged hedge funds, and which has shown itself as hospitable to crony capitalism as anywhere in the world.

No doubt American capitalism will renew itself, as it has done in the past. American business has never operated within the narrow confines of free market models. Even so, the universal claims of the most recent version of American capitalism are damaged beyond repair. This is only a return to reality. All economic systems are flawed. All go through cycles of decline and rebirth. None has the ability to replicate itself everywhere.

Capitalism grows in many varieties. Economic activity is not a freestanding form of social life. It is an outgrowth of the religious beliefs, family relationships and national traditions in which it is embedded. Business enterprises operate differently in Eastern Orthodox societies from the way they do in Catholic societies; Chinese capitalism is quite different from Japanese capitalism, Hindu from Muslim. There are many hybrids. As they modernise, the varieties of capitalism will not become more alike. They will renew themselves in different ways. No economic system is uniquely adapted to the changing conditions of the modern world.

There was never any prospect of the many varieties of capitalism being replaced by a pallid Anglo-Saxon monoculture. Yet, for a time, American policies were shaped by the belief that such a world-historical transformation was not only inevitable but also imminent. US policies were based on the belief that cultural differences are surface manifestations of economic forces that will disappear, or else shrink into insignificance, with the advance of knowledge and technology – a view strikingly reminiscent of Marxian determinism. As Liah Greenfeld has observed: 'Curiously, Marxism, abandoned in the lands traditionally dedicated to its propagation and proved wrong by experience, is remarkably similar to the Anglo-American view of the world.'[16]

America's neo-liberal missionaries embraced the weakest aspects of Marx's thought. They emulated his historical determinism, but lacked his Homeric vision of historical conflict. Marx knew that capitalism is endemically unstable. His American followers imagined it had reached an equilibrium that would last forever. Marx perceived that capitalism was destroying bourgeois life. His American disciples were confident that bourgeois life would soon be universal.

The sub-Marxian, neo-liberal worldview that shaped American policies in the Nineties could not last. Well before the terrorist attacks the US was losing interest in globalisation. Later, when President Bush imposed tariffs on steel and farm products, it became clear that maintaining the global free market was no longer a priority. It is probably only a matter of time before the US thumbs its nose at the World Trade Organisation. In that event, trade will return to being a matter of bilateral negotiations among governments and blocs. The international system will revert to being a society of sovereign states.

From being the pacemaker of globalisation, the US has opted for globalisation in one country. The risk is that the sea change in American policy will result in a contraction of world trade. At worst, tit-for-tat protectionism could lead to a rerun of something like the Great Depression. In any event, it is the US that has brought the neo-liberal experiment to a close. No doubt the attacks of September 11th spurred the shift in American policies, but they were well underway before then. The Bush administration will go down in history as the gravedigger of the global free market.

From one side, the global free market depended on a continuing American commitment to free trade. From another, it required that foreign investors continue to accept American capitalism as a universal model. When these conditions broke down, the global free market began to fall apart.

5

Geopolitics and the limits of growth

> When all the world is overcharged with inhabitants,
> then the last remedy of all is war; which provideth for every
> man, by victory, or death.
>
> Thomas Hobbes[1]

The post-Cold War era was an interregnum between two eras of conflict. With the end of its ideological disputes, older sources of rivalry and enmity have re-emerged. The world has returned to a condition in some ways like that which existed towards the end of the nineteenth century, when the chief focus of war and diplomacy was control of natural resources.

The economic theory that underpins the global free market rejects the very idea of resource-scarcity. If demand exceeds supply, resources will become expensive. As a result, new supplies will be found, or technological alternatives developed. In this view, so long as market pricing is in place and technological innovation continues, economic growth cannot be derailed by scarcity. For all practical purposes, natural resources are infinite.

The idea that human invention can overcome natural scarcity is not new. The Positivists believed that industrialisation would enable humanity to conquer scarcity.

Following them in this faith, Karl Marx imagined that industrialism would make possible a condition of abundance in which both markets and the state would be obsolete. Herbert Spencer – an almost unknown thinker today, but one who was extremely influential at the start of the twentieth century – shared Marx's vision, maintaining that industrialism made war an anachronism.[2]

Before Marx, the belief that human ingenuity could overcome scarcity had long been a mainstay of utopian thought. Charles Fourier is reputed to have believed that a time would come when the oceans would be made of lemonade. The early nineteenth-century French utopian thinker has suffered unending ridicule, but his prognostications were no more far-fetched than those of late twentieth-century free-market economists.

Like Marxists, neo-liberals imagine that with the triumph of industrialisation there will be no more wars of scarcity. They forget that industrial societies depend for their survival on energy sources that are not fungible. Once used, they cannot be used again. The most important among them – oil – is distributed very unevenly throughout the world. The same is true of fresh water. As worldwide industrialisation proceeds, competition for these resources is bound to intensify.

Despite the fact that the twentieth century witnessed larger and more destructive wars than any in history, the belief that industrialisation and peace advance together has not been abandoned. The majority of economists have followed Marx and Spencer in thinking that industrialism had consigned natural scarcity to the past. In the

1970s, the Club of Rome showed that finite natural resources could not support exponentially rising population and production. It failed to dent the faith that industrial societies had discovered the secret of perpetual growth.[3]

History outran the prescience of economists. By the 1990s resource-scarcity was a source of war. The Gulf War was waged to prevent Kuwaiti and Saudi oil supplies falling out of western control. A decade later control of energy supplies dominated strategic thinking. Well before September 11th, the Bush administration made clear that it regarded access to energy as a matter of national security. In the aftermath of the attacks, the US concluded a far-reaching rapprochement with Russia whose centrepiece was joint exploitation of the energy resources of Central Asia. The Great Game has resumed.

The limits to growth have not disappeared. They have returned as geopolitics. Twenty-first century wars will be resource wars, made more dangerous and intractable by being intertwined with ethnic and religious enmities.

Far from resource scarcity fading away with economic development, ongoing industrialisation is making it a pivotal source of conflict. The best guide to these emerging conflicts is geography. In the Middle East and southern Asia, water is a major source of conflict: 'The Jordan River Basin flows through Israel, Jordan, Lebanon, Syria and Palestinian territory; the Tigris–Euphrates system passes through Iran, Iraq, Syria, Turkey and areas occupied by the Kurdish population; and the Indus is shared among Afghanistan, China, Pakistan and Kashmir (some of whose inhabitants seek to become independent). These countries and religions are deeply divided along political, religious, ethnic and ideological lines. Disputes about water are therefore likely to be intensified by historical grievances and animosities.'[4]

Conflict over water was a factor in the twentieth century's last big genocide. In less than a generation, the population of Rwanda more than tripled. In 1992, the country had the highest population growth rate in the world, with an average of eight children for every woman. Food production could not keep pace. Water was heavily overdrawn. War between the Hutu and the Tutsi had a number of causes; but it soon became a struggle for water, in which around two million people were killed.[5]

Rivalry for scarce natural resources played a central role in the twentieth century's largest wars. Competition for oil supplies was a formative influence on the Second World War. A US embargo on oil exports to Japan was the deciding factor in tipping the balance of opinion in the Japanese military in favour of war. The prospect of seizing Soviet oil production facilities was a major factor in Hitler's decision to invade Russia in 1941. If history is any guide, the coming century will be punctuated by oil wars.

Today, competition for shrinking supplies of hydrocarbons underpins every major potential conflict. The last great pools of cheap conventional oil – around two thirds of the world's known reserves of petroleum – lie in the Persian Gulf. In former Soviet Central Asia, the great powers are vying for control of the Caspian Basin's large reserves of petroleum and natural gas. In the South China

Sea, underwater oil deposits in the Spratly Islands are claimed by China, Taiwan, Vietnam, the Philippines and Malaysia. Each of these three regions is the site of an arms race.

Behind intensifying rivalries for natural resources are increasing human numbers. Continued population growth worldwide increases the human impact on the planet as a whole. The result is increasing geopolitical conflict.

Thomas Malthus is commonly seen as a false prophet who failed to appreciate the power of human invention in defeating scarcity. In fact he uttered a forbidden truth. Like other animals, humans can overshoot the carrying capacity of their environment. When that happens, famine, plague or war will cull their numbers. At no time in history has this truth been more salient. As Robert Kaplan has written:

Malthus – the first philosopher to focus on the political effects of poor soils, famine, disease, and the quality of life among the poor – is an irritant because he has defined the most important debate of the first half of the twenty-first century. As the human population rises from six billion to ten billion before it is predicted to level off, testing the planet's environment as never before – with a billion people going hungry and violence (both political and criminal) chronic throughout poor parts of the globe – the word Malthusian will be heard with increasing frequency in the years to come.[6]

For Marxists and neo-liberals alike, there can never be too many people.[7] Yet poor countries know that there is an imbalance between expanding populations and scarce resources. China, Egypt, Iran and India all have population policies. Their efforts to control their numbers are viewed with indifference or hostility in the West. This is only natural. What could be more convenient for the West than a world abounding in cheap labour? Remember Voltaire's quip: 'The comfort of the rich depends on abundant supply of the poor.'[8]

The comfort of the rich comes with a price. Fertility is falling in Europe and Japan, and in European Russia it has collapsed; but in other parts of the world human numbers are rising fast. The theory of demographic transition tells us that population growth trails off as a side effect of rising prosperity. As usual, this economic explanation neglects cultural factors. In nearly all countries, it is not affluence that lowers population growth. It is control of their fertility by women. Where contraception and abortion are easily available human numbers level off, and then fall. Where they are discouraged there is no such demographic transition. In such circumstances, geopolitical upheaval is unavoidable.

Nowhere is this clearer than in the Persian Gulf, where traditional values and the growing power of radical Islam deny access to contraception. When incomes were rising in the region, population grew rapidly. Now that they are falling it is growing just as fast. At present the doubling rate of Gulf State populations is around twenty years.[9]

The countries of the Gulf are not starving; but within a generation they will face a Malthusian crisis in which escalating human needs run up against dwindling natural resources. They are *rentier* economies that rely on a single depleting commodity. Within the lifetimes of people who are now young adults, the oil reserves of the Gulf will peak. At that point, population can be expected also to peak.[10]

The growing populations of the Gulf need high or rising oil prices. The US, Europe, Japan, China and India need stable or falling oil prices. In itself, this could be a manageable conflict; but it coincides with a steep rise in fundamentalism. Rising population and falling incomes are fuelling anti-western movements. It is not easy to envisage a scenario in which these conflicts are peacefully resolved.

The position is starkest in Saudi Arabia. On some estimates, per capita income in that country has fallen by around three quarters over the past twenty years. Some of this is due to falling oil prices, but much of it is a result of population growth. As the population doubles over the next twenty years per capita income could fall by as much again. At present almost 50 per cent of Saudis are under fifteen. Large numbers of young males face unemployment. Most of these have been schooled to view the West with deep suspicion. The combination of an expanding population and falling living standards with a fundamentalist education system renders the Saudi regime inherently unstable.

The situation in the Gulf marks a global shift. Population growth is high in Islamic countries. This trend could accelerate as a result of the differential impact of AIDS.

The devastating effects that AIDS is having in central and southern Africa look set to be replicated in Russia, where nearly all of the factors favouring its rapid transmission –

high levels of promiscuity and prostitution, pandemic intravenous drug use and poor medical services – are present. The population of European Russia will be more than decimated. Some years after that, India and China are likely to suffer a similar die-off.

The situation of Islamic countries seems markedly different. To the extent that their repressive sexual codes are actually enforced they close one key portal that allows AIDS to spread. In this respect, Islamic cultures – particularly the most puritanical – may have an advantage over most others. If so, epidemic disease will re-emerge as one of the forces shaping history.[11]

In terms of global population the impact of AIDS is slight. Even on the most conservative projections, the world's human population will increase by around two billion over the next fifty years. At the same time, industrialisation is spreading rapidly. One result is much higher energy consumption worldwide.

In the West the geopolitical risks that go with rising global energy use are little recognised. In China they are well understood. Over the next two decades, China will join the US and Japan and become one of the world's largest oil importers.[12] The stresses this will create have been summarised by Professor Ji Guoxing, Director of the Institute of Strategy Studies in Shanghai:

The world energy equation is not promising, and oil supply prospects in world oil markets are not optimistic. World oil production will begin to decline before 2010, sooner than most people think, and oil prices would then rise in real terms. It is predicted that around 2010 a perpetual global oil shortage will seem certain. Unlike previous shocks, it will not be a short-term supply interruption, but will herald a historic discontinuity with profound implications for both the oil industry and oil consumers . . . The views traditionally held in economic circles that 'so long as there is demand, there is supply' and 'the world might never run out of oil' are dangerous and incompatible with the truth . . . Economists assert that higher prices will endlessly refill petroleum reserves by granting incentives to produce. This was true in the 1970s, when price controls discouraged production; it may not be true after 2010, when feasible reserves begin to decline . . . The effect of energy rivalries and tension could easily have destabilising international and regional consequences.[13]

Economists will dispute this assessment. If the price mechanism is allowed to operate, they will claim, new technology will displace oil as the chief source of energy for industrial economies, rendering natural scarcity irrelevant.

Two facts preclude this happy outcome. In the first place, technology cannot repeal the laws of thermodynamics. Market pricing can enhance financial returns as oil becomes scarcer, but only up to a point. When the energy costs of extracting oil exceed the energy thereby produced, no price can make the process profitable. There is nothing to be done about this. It is a consequence of the universal fact of entropy.[14]

Oil is a gift of the sun. Laid down billions of years ago, global reserves are now peaking. True, over the past seventy years, new technologies have continually enabled new hydrocarbon reserves to be found, including natural gas. Oil reserves have been extended by deep underwater exploration, or by drilling beneath the polar ice. Yet a time will come when the energy that available hydrocarbons contain will be too low in quality to be worth extracting. Despite all technical advances, these resources are unalterably finite.

The second fact standing in the way of a technical fix for energy shortage is the urgency of human needs. Oil depletion may not be an imminent danger, but in only a few decades it could be a reality.[15] Modern industrial societies run on hydrocarbons. Intensive agriculture is the extraction of food from petroleum. Looking ahead, governments know that economic survival may depend on control of oil reserves. Their fear of this prospect stands behind the emerging conflicts in the Gulf, the Caspian Basin and the South China Sea. It also explains the growing American interest in Africa, where there are sizeable oil reserves.

When the necessities of life are at stake, humans will not wait for technical innovation or the market to operate. They will demand – and obtain – political action. The price mechanism is a creature of state power. It operates only so long as the state is intact. When scarcity amounts to a threat to subsistence, market pricing breaks down. The state becomes an instrument of rationing or conquest.

Increasing resource scarcity would be dangerous even if the global environment were stable. In fact it is increasingly unstable. The geopolitical risks of resource scarcity are being aggravated by climate change.

Technology can spin out natural resources. It cannot stop climate change. Partly caused by greenhouse gas emissions in the past, it is a process that cannot now be arrested. Insofar as it is humanly caused, global warming is a by-product of worldwide industrialisation. The emergence of China and India as industrial powers will accelerate climatic changes that are already irreversible.[16]

Over the coming century, global warming may well overtake scarcity in energy supplies as a source of geopolitical conflict. In some areas it means desertification; in others flood. Food production is likely to be disrupted. Densely populated coastal countries such as Bangladesh could be inundated. These changes in the physical landscape will trigger large movements of population, as people attempt to flee to zones of safety.

By the end of the Nineties flows of people from regions devastated by war, failed states or ecological collapse were generating acute political controversy in many of the world's rich, well-governed states. These asylum seekers and economic refugees attest to a central contradiction in the global free market.

In an earlier era of globalisation from 1870 to the outbreak of the First World War, the free movement of capital was combined with freedom of migration. In Europe only Russia and Turkey required passports for travel into the country. Late twentieth-century globalisation is different. Free capital flows coexist with stringent restrictions on flows of people. By the late Nineties, this combination was leading to large-scale illegal immigration.

This contrast between the two eras of globalisation is explained by political changes, some of them highly desirable. In the late nineteenth century, democracy was limited in most European countries and their colonies; the welfare state was nonexistent; and trade unions were weak. At the end of the twentieth century, democracy was entrenched throughout Europe, as were trade unions and the welfare state. In these circumstances, immigrants were easily perceived as a threat. Politicians reacted by proposing ever more severe restrictions on the movement of people.

Democracy has numerous advantages, but in a time of globalisation it has some awkward consequences. In some European countries, far right parties have succeeded in shaping the political agenda, or even entering national government, by playing on the racist fears of voters. Even where the far right is not a major political force, competition among mainstream parties has resulted in policies that curb the flow of people. In the aftermath of the attacks on Washington and New York, these constraints on free movement have intensified.

The tension between free flows of capital and restrictions on the movement of people can only be made more acute by climate change. The poor who seek to migrate from the world's collapsed zones will find their exit blocked. Strongly governed countries will use the powers of the state to throw up barriers to flows of people.

At the beginning of the twenty-first century, the pattern of global conflict is shaped by population growth, shrinking energy supplies and irreversible climate change. Together with ethnic and religious enmities and the collapse or corrosion of the state in many parts of the world, these forces are changing the nature of war.

6

The metamorphosis of war

> If you go back to the birth of nations, if you come down to
> our own day, if you examine peoples in all possible conditions
> from the state of barbarism to the most advanced
> civilization, you always find war.
>
> Joseph de Maistre[1]

The medieval world recognised many authorities, none absolute. The Treaty of Westphalia introduced a new actor into the law of nations: the sovereign state, whose authority within its own borders is unlimited. With the invention of the modern state, authority was located for the first time in a single institution. At the same time, the state claimed a legal monopoly of organised violence, and war between states came to be seen as the model for all types of military conflict.[2]

For Carl von Clausewitz, a Prussian officer who founded the modern theory of war in intervals between active military service with the end of the Napoleonic Wars and the Peace of Vienna in 1815, war meant armed conflict between states. The pattern of organised violence that prevailed before 1648 was irrelevant. In practice, the state's monopoly of violence was far from complete even in Europe at the time Clausewitz's treatise *On War* was published in 1832.[3] In many European countries, the state's writ did not run very far. Most European governments did not possess an effective monopoly of force until after the First World War. Even so, Clausewitz was right to see the future of war in terms of conflicts between states. From the Napoleonic wars until the Soviet collapse, the armed conflicts that ravaged Europe and the world were mostly duels between governments.

Clausewitz was a powerfully influential thinker, not only in military strategy but also in social theory. Max Weber followed him in thinking that a monopoly of organised violence is the defining power of the modern state. For Weber, the spread of the modern state was a part of the diffusion of rational modes of thinking promoted by science.

By the last decade of the twentieth century, this Weberian view of the state was at least partly obsolete. In many parts of the world its monopoly of violence had broken down. Weapons of mass destruction were at risk of leaking out of the control of governments. The diffusion of science and technology had not advanced modern states. It had produced a new type of warfare, unforeseen by Weber or Clausewitz.

In the Middle East and the Balkans, Kashmir and Afghanistan and other zones of conflict, it is not only states and their agents who are waging war. Central amongst the protagonists are political organisations, irregular militias and fundamentalist networks that are not controlled by any state. That does not mean Clausewitzian war has disappeared. The Falklands War and the Gulf War were wars between states. In future, it is not inconceivable that great powers will once again go to war against one another. But today many of the most intractable conflicts are post-Clausewitzian wars.

Unconventional warfare involving the targeting of government personnel and civilian populations has been practised in Vietnam, Angola, Malaya, Northern Ireland, the Basque country, Sri Lanka, Israel, Algeria and many other places. What is new about the kind of unconventional warfare that emerged in the Nineties is that it has developed in the context of corroded or failed states.

Political thinkers have neglected the collapse of the state across much of the world.[4] Yet it is a fact that hundreds of millions of people are living in conditions of semi-anarchy. In much of Africa, parts of post-communist Russia, in Afghanistan and Pakistan, in Latin American countries such as Colombia and Haiti and in regions of Europe such as Bosnia and Kosovo, Chechnya and Albania, there is nothing resembling an effective modern state.

In these countries, it is not so much that civil war has left the state weakened as that failed states have become the normal condition. In such semi-anarchy, the protagonists to armed conflict continuously shift and split, form new alliances and acquire new enemies. Peace cannot simply be declared. If it is achievable at all, it is only as a precarious balance of forces, liable to break down at any time.

Unconventional warfare of the kind practised by Al Qaeda has its breeding grounds in the zones of anarchy that flow from failed states, but it thrives on the weakness of the state in another way. As capital has gone global, so has crime. Nearly everywhere, the irregular armies and political organisations that practise the new forms of warfare are linked with the global criminal economy. Many terrorist organisations rely for some of their funding on crime, particularly the trade in illegal drugs. With globalisation, they are able to move the funds they acquire from these sources freely around the world. Al Qaeda has taken full advantage of this freedom.[5]

The debility of the state is partly a result of deliberate policy. In the go-go years of the Nineties, state power was seen as a remnant of collectivism. A roll-back of government was promoted as a vital condition of 'market reform'. In practice, dismantling controls on the flow of capital created a casino capitalism in which the economies of countries such as Thailand and Indonesia could be wrecked by sudden large outflows of speculative capital. At the same time, the freedom of capital flows from political control created a vast pool of offshore wealth in which the funds of terrorist organisations can vanish without trace.

The attack on the state in the Nineties facilitated terrorism in yet another way. As the Soviet state fell apart, many thousands of research scientists in the vast military-industrial complex became unemployed or destitute. As these casualties of a botched transition struggled to keep afloat, weapons and materials passed into the hands of criminal mafias. If there is now an increased risk of terrorists using weapons of mass destruction, it is partly a consequence of

74

the policies imposed by western governments on post-communist Russia, which aggravated the weakness of an already enfeebled state.

Terrorism thrives on the weakness of states. This is not to say that states have had no role in sponsoring it. Links between governments and terrorists are meant to be indecipherable. Even so, it is known that countries such as Somalia, Sudan and Guinea-Bissau have allowed Al Qaeda to take refuge in them. The Taliban regime that harboured Al Qaeda in Afghanistan appears to have been largely constructed from Saudi funding by sections of Pakistan's intelligence agencies.

Despite these links, Al Qaeda is not the instrument of any government. None has much leverage over its activities. Partly for that reason, it has long been an object of suspicion on the part of states such as Iraq.[6]

Today, as in the past, most terrorism is national or regional in its scope and goals. Even if their funds are scattered across the world, organisations such as ETA in the Basque country of Spain, the IRA in Ulster, the Tamil Tigers in Sri Lanka and the PLO in Gaza remain based in one or a few countries. Moreover, their objectives are local.

In contrast, Al Qaeda is global in its activities. It has a proven capacity to strike in any part of the world. That is not so say Al Qaeda's strategic goals are essentially global. Its strategic objective has always been more concrete and limited – the overthrow of the House of Saud. In pursuing that regional goal, however, it has been drawn into a worldwide conflict with American power.

Al Qaeda has a clear understanding of the vulnerabilities of western industrial societies. By destroying the Saudi regime, it will eject infidels from sacred soil. By gaining control of Saudi oil it will hold the industrialised world to ransom. The logic of its strategic goals requires that its reach be worldwide.

'Al Qaeda is an essentially modern organisation.'[7] It is modern not only in the fact that it uses satellite phones, laptop computers and encrypted websites. The attack on the Twin Towers demonstrates that Al Qaeda understands that twenty-first century wars are spectacular encounters in which the dissemination of media images is a core strategy. Its use of satellite television to mobilise support in Muslim countries is part of this strategy.

It is not only in its use of communication technologies that Al Qaeda is modern. So is its organisation. Al Qaeda resembles less the centralised command structures of twentieth-century revolutionary parties than the cellular structures of drug cartels and the flattened networks of virtual business corporations. Without fixed abode and with active members from practically every part of the world, Al Qaeda is 'a global multinational'.[8]

The origins of Al Qaeda ('The Base') are in the Cold War. It developed in the late 1980s during the struggle against the Soviet invasion of Afghanistan that was orchestrated by the US, Saudi Arabia and European governments. On the basis of the operational structures it inherited from that time, it became the first practitioner of unconventional warfare to be truly worldwide in its operations. Al Qaeda is 'the first multinational terrorist organisation, capable of functioning from Latin America to Japan and all the other continents in between. Unlike the terrorists of the 1970s and 1980s, Al Qaeda is not guided by territorial jurisdiction – its theatre of support, as well as its operations, is global. Instead of resisting globalisation, its forces are being harnessed by contemporary Islamist groups, constantly looking for new bases and new targets worldwide.'[9]

Al Qaeda's ideology is a typical modern hybrid. Though they claim to be exponents of an indigenous tradition, its founders have reinterpreted Islam in the light of contemporary western thought. At the King Abdul Aziz university in Jeddah, Osama Bin Laden was taught Islamic studies by Muhammad Qutb, the brother of Sayyid Qutb, the ideologue who more than anyone else invented radical Islam. In some ways more moderate than his brother, Muhammad Qutb nevertheless shared with him the belief that the West was suffering from a 'great spiritual famine'. He passed on this conviction to Osama bin Laden.[10]

Less may be known about the character of Osama bin Laden than is commonly believed. Born in Riyadh, Saudi Arabia, the seventeenth son of fifty-two children in a family of four wives and numerous concubines, Osama was his mother's only son. His father – a wealthy businessman specialising in large construction projects – came from the Hadhramaut, a region in the protectorate of Aden, now the Republic of Yemen, that has long been involved in international trade. His mother was a Syrian, who was divorced by her husband soon after Osama's birth. It is said that Osama resented the low status accorded by the family to his mother, and by implication to him. It is also said that, reared in luxury, bin Laden lived the life of a playboy in his youth, enjoying the freedoms of Lebanon whilst studying there and acquiring 'a conspicuous canary-yellow Mercedes SL 450, with burnt-orange interior, air conditioning, cruise control and electric windows'.[11]

The accuracy of such reports is hard to assess. What seems fairly clear is that, like Sayyid Qutb and many radical Islamists, bin Laden reacted strongly against the hedonism and individualism of western life. Living for a time in the relatively westernised culture of Lebanon bred contempt for secular values. On his return to Saudi Arabia, bin Laden seems to have had something like a conversion experience in which he re-embraced Islam. He did not thereby become an Islamist intellectual. From the first he saw the struggle against the West in military terms. The man who is commonly identified with Al Qaeda did not originate it. His contribution was that of an organiser and tactician. As Gunaratna has written: '[Bin Laden] is not an original thinker but an opportunist, a businessman at heart, who surrounds himself with a good team, manages it well but borrows heavily from others.'[12]

The thinker who most shaped bin Laden's views, and who drew up Al Qaeda's founding charter in 1987–8, was Dr Abdullah Azzam. A Jordanian Palestinian and doctor of Islamic jurisprudence, 'the most influential of all the exponents of the modern jihadist movement'[13] and one of the architects of Hamas, Azzam was instrumental with bin Laden in setting up the Afghan Service Bureau, an organisation that assisted the *mujahidin* in Afghanistan. Azzam and bin Laden were pivotal figures in the struggle against the Soviet occupation of Afghanistan. Bin Laden had left Saudi Arabia within weeks of the Soviet invasion in December 1979, joining up with the commanders of the anti-Soviet *jihad* in a multinational coalition organised by the CIA that included Britain, Saudi Arabia, China and several other countries. For many years Azzam was bin Laden's intellectual mentor, but they fell out over issues of strategy. In 1989 Azzam was murdered in a bombing that also killed his two sons, an assassination in which bin Laden has been implicated.[14]

As elaborated by Azzam, Al Qaeda's ideology is a highly syncretic construction. Azzam took from Qutb the idea of a revolutionary vanguard – a notion whose affiliations are more with Bolshevik ideology than with any Islamic source. His attack on rationalism contains echoes of Nietzsche. Modern western influences are fused with Islamic themes.

A glimpse of Al Qaeda's ideology in action was provided by the Taliban regime, over which bin Laden had considerable influence through his friendship with its leader Mullah Omar. Women were forced out of employment and education. Homosexuality was punishable by burial under a 15-foot brick wall. Policies such as these are described as medieval, but the Taliban had more in common with Pol Pot. When the Taliban shelled the ancient statues of the Buddha at Bamiyan at the instigation of bin Laden in March 2000, it aimed to destroy a treasure that had outlasted many traditional regimes.[15]

Al Qaeda is a sufficiently resilient network to survive

and function well in the event of the death or incapacity of its leader. That does not mean it cannot be disabled. Its structure may be like that of the Internet, as is often claimed, but in that case it is vulnerable. The Internet is clustered around a small number of key nodes. If these are disabled the system fails. The same may be true of Al Qaeda.

How far Al Qaeda has been damaged in the American-led 'war on terror' cannot be known. What seems clear is that it has a formidable capacity for self-renewal. One reason for this is that its structure mirrors social forms that are conventionally viewed as pre-modern.

Al Qaeda is organised on the model of an extended family. Using the ties of trust that bind families together, it can make considerable use of informal banking systems (*hawala*) that are global in their reach and whose operations are effectively untraceable. Its clannish structure makes it extremely difficult to penetrate. The deep commitment fostered by Al Qaeda's familial structure enables it to mount long-term missions such as the attacks on American embassies in Africa, which were preceded by years of patient preparation.

Al Qaeda's 'pre-modern values' enable it to operate very effectively in conditions of globalisation. In fact, of course, they are not pre-modern. Individualist values are found in England, Scotland and the United States during the modern period, but they are only one strand in the complex pattern of attitudes and practices through which these societies came to modernity. In the Scottish case, modern capitalism was rooted in extended family networks; the global reach of Scottish merchant adventurers was made possible by continuing family traditions. Even in the English and American examples, modern capitalism may have developed from a form of collective identity – nationalism. This seems a distinct possibility in the case of Imperial Germany, which was certainly a modern society, but never unequivocally committed to individualist values. Modernity cannot be equated with the emergence of individualism. Even in the western heartlands of modernity, there has always been more than one way of being modern.[16]

It is sometimes argued that Al Qaeda is not much different from the terrorist movements of the past, such as the communist insurgents the British defeated in Malaya in the Fifties. In this view, the proper response to September 11th is not to prepare for war. The answer to terrorism is a form of police action. Despite its impressive credentials,[17] this view is misguided.

The attacks of September 11th were certainly acts of terror, but they were not ordinary terrorism. They demonstrated that unconventional warfare had escalated to a global level. In contrast, the Malayan communists were a danger in Malaya, but they remained a local force. They never attempted a campaign in Britain. Despite the fact that much of the fighting took place in jungle conditions, the insurgents were concentrated in a territory over which the British state had a high level of control. Al Qaeda is a world network, with outposts in regions that no state controls.

The attacks on New York and Washington were acts of

war – but not war of a conventional kind. They were examples of asymmetric warfare, in which the weak seek out and exploit the vulnerabilities of the strong. Using civilian airplanes as weapons and its operatives as delivery systems, Al Qaeda demonstrated that despite the 'revolution in military affairs' (RMA) that has given America an unchallengeable military superiority over all other states, the US remains vulnerable to devastating attack.[18]

The core of RMA is the use of highly sophisticated computer sensor devices, whereby the fog of war can be lifted and commanders enabled to view the combat situation clearly and respond with high-precision (often unmanned) weapons. These technologies are expensive, and available only to the richest states. They can be highly effective in disabling known enemies – as was demonstrated when an American missile from an unmanned drone, operated at great distance, killed a senior Al Qaeda operative in the Yemen in November 2002. They cannot prevent attacks such as occurred on September 11th. At the same time, cheaper technologies are enhancing the potential destructiveness of unconventional warfare.

Nuclear materials are hard to obtain and dangerous to use; but when deployed by suicide bombers they provide the rudiments of radiological weapons that can inflict mass casualties. Bio-weapons are also dangerous to use, but the knowledge and materials needed to make them are widely available, and scientific advance is making them ever more deadly. Some weapons are sufficiently long acting to make their origins practically untraceable. Genetically selective weapons allow the targeting of specific populations. It is hard to estimate the risk of Al Qaeda using these radiological and biological capabilities; but by seeking to acquire them they have transcended ordinary terrorism.

There is a growing risk of cyber-terrorism. The spread of advanced computer skills among the soldiers of stateless armies creates the potential for a type of cyber war directed at civilian targets such as airports and power stations as well as military command structures. Other types of cyber-attack are feasible. Using sophisticated hacking techniques, the Zapatista rebels in Mexico have disrupted financial markets. There have been reports that Al Qaeda has made similar attempts. The growth of the cyber-economy creates a new battlefield for unconventional warfare.

In prosecuting this new kind of war Al Qaeda has the strength that comes with its rejection of individualism. The relationships of trust on which its organisation can rely, and the willingness of its operatives to go to certain death, give it a powerful advantage. Liberal societies cannot replicate this suicidal solidarity. Values of personal choice and self-realisation are too deeply encrypted in them. Even so, they are bound to defend themselves. Using new technologies of electronic eavesdropping, face-recognition and the like, modern liberal states are acquiring unprecedented powers of surveillance over the populations within their borders. In an effort to track the potential terrorists in their midst, they are subjecting the entire population to high levels of monitoring. The price of individualism is proving to be the loss of privacy.

Modern war is a by-product of the modern state. For a

long time modern states waged limited wars. In the Napoleonic Wars, conscription – the *levée en masse* – was employed to raise mass armies; but on the whole civilian populations were not targeted. With the First World War, conscription became universal; the entire economy was mobilised for the war effort; civilian populations came to be viewed as legitimate targets. In this respect, liberal regimes showed themselves to be fully as ruthless as total-itarian states. In order to defend democracy against dicta-torship in the Second World War, the civilian populations of Dresden and Hamburg, Hiroshima, Nagasaki and Tokyo were incinerated.

The aftermath of September 11th has produced a new kind of unlimited war. The Hobbesian anarchy that flows from failed states has enabled stateless armies to strike into the heart of the world's greatest power. In response, the US and other liberal regimes are turning themselves into Hobbesian surveillance states.

7

Pax Americana?

The American insistence that human freedom implies history's
malleability has engendered an activist foreign policy which
presumes that nations and international society can be changed
into something more acceptable to Americans. This is the sense
of the American Century: that in it history has been achieving
its democratic fulfilment. It is the American temper to force
matters to a conclusion, to settle, win, put it all behind, move on
to something else. It is crucially hard to accept that history does
not have a stop: that there are problems at the heart of American
national security that might have no solution.

William Pfaff[1]

During the twelve years between the fall of the Berlin Wall
and the destruction of the Twin Towers, successive
American administrations used their control over institutions such as the IMF to construct a financial empire. Al
Qaeda's actions demonstrated that a paper empire is no
protection against resolute foes.

Since September 11th, the Bush administration has
erected more tangible defences. Defence spending has
been boosted. Great-power diplomacy has been revived,
notably with Russia, China and India. A new strategic doctrine of pre-emption has been announced. Animating all
these initiatives is a belief that the world can be made safe

by a Pax Americana in which America's global hegemony is entrenched for the foreseeable future.

If there is to be a global hegemonic power, it must be the US. But is Pax Americana feasible? Has America the will to take on the burdens it brings and the restraint to make it work?

In conventional military terms America is already the sole mega-power. US American defence spending exceeds that of many other powers combined. Movements in exchange rates complicate the calculation, but American defence expenditure in 2003 could well match that of the next dozen or more defence budgets. US military superiority is not only a matter of the huge resources it has committed to defence. It has an unbridgeable technical lead over any other power. If it cooperates less and less with other countries in military operations, one reason is that its technologies are too advanced to be interoperable with those of lesser powers.

Pax Americana demands much more than this technological primacy. First, it presupposes that the US has the economic strength to support the imperial role it entails. Second, it assumes that the US has the will to sustain it. Third, it requires that the rest of the world be ready to accept it. It is questionable whether any of these conditions can be met.

In considering the first of these three conditions a comparison with the British Empire may be useful. At the height of its imperial power, when a quarter of the world's population lived under British rule, Britain was the world's biggest capital exporter. Between 1870 and 1913,

the proportion of British wealth that was invested overseas rose from 17 per cent to 33 per cent – far higher than
any other country at the time.[2] In contrast, the US has
used its geopolitical dominance to secure investment in
US markets. As a result, it is the world's largest importer
of capital. While using its hegemonic power in this way, it
has limited its freedom of action in foreign policy: 'you
cannot have "dollar diplomacy" without dollars. In short,
the global hegemony of the present age of globalisation
has much less financial leverage than that of the first
age.'[3]

During the interregnum between the end of the Cold
War and the terrorist attacks, these financial restraints on
American foreign policy were masked. American markets
attracted foreign investment on a vast scale. Today their
appeal is muted.

Foreign investors are not only distrustful of the rates of
return promised by American companies and nervous
about the future of the dollar. Some of them – particularly
the Saudis, who have a pivotal role in global financial markets – are deeply hostile to American foreign policy. The
risk that large amounts of capital will be withdrawn from
American markets on these grounds may not be great.
Countries that encouraged such a withdrawal might well
face American retaliation. Moreover, large-scale capital
flight from the US would precipitate a global financial crisis. It is unclear that any other country is ready to trigger
such an outcome.

Even so, the situation of the US is quite different from
that which existed a decade or so ago. Then America's

allies paid for the Gulf War. Today, if the US wishes to launch pre-emptive attacks on 'rogue states' it will have to pay for them itself.

The Nineties boom concealed a fundamental ambiguity in America's position in the world. It is the sole military mega-power; but its ability to project its military power worldwide depends on its economic primacy, which has been eroding for decades. This hidden weakness will surely be exposed in coming years.

The costs of American hegemonic role are not only financial. They include casualties. Unless the US can persuade other countries to act on its behalf, it must be willing to accept a steady flow of body bags as part of the price of shaping global security on its terms. Historically, Americans have been reluctant to 'act as the world's policeman'. The attacks of September 11th may have shown them that they no longer have the option of isolation. But are they willing to pay the blood price of empire?

September 11th was an example of globally organised resistance to US power. Such a threat requires a global response. After Al Qaeda's attacks, the US cannot avoid engaging in an open-ended encounter with a world that rejects many of its core values.

There is another reason why America cannot withdraw from the world. It is too dependent on imported oil. Heavy overseas military commitments flow inexorably from America's profligate use of energy.

If Al Qaeda were to achieve its goal of overturning the Saudi regime it would have a stranglehold over the American economy. True, the US may be able to reduce its dependency on Saudi oil; but in the short to medium run of the next few decades it can do so only by deepening its involvement in other oil-producing regions. The strategic rapprochement with Russia over the resources of the Caspian Basin requires a continuing military presence. So will Iraq in the aftermath of a change of regime resulting from any American-led military intervention.

Isolation is not possible, but there are several reasons why America is unready to assume the role of a global imperial power. The chief among these is not America's self-image as an anti-colonial nation. That has not prevented the US engaging in imperial interventions in Latin America and elsewhere. Rather, the obstacle is an unresolved ambiguity in American perceptions of the world.

There is nothing resembling a uniquely American worldview. America is too vast, and ultimately too unknowable, to give birth to one way of seeing things. Despite this, there are some common American beliefs and attitudes.

On the one hand, many Americans believe that all human beings are Americans under the skin. On the other hand, they have long viewed the world – especially the Old World of Europe – as corrupt, possibly beyond redemption. In the past, the first of these attitudes has supported a global role, as when the US entered Europe's two twentieth-century civil wars, sponsoring policies of national self-determination after World War One and the Marshall Plan after World War Two. The second has nurtured isolation.

Contradictory as these American attitudes seem, they

flow from a common premise. Either the world will evolve to the point at which it mirrors America, or else it can safely be left to its own devices. Al Qaeda has destroyed this assumption.

The ambiguity in American perceptions is mirrored in the strategy of pre-empting threats. From one angle, it is an attempt to secure the US from attack. From another, it is one more effort to remake the world in an American image.

The new American defence doctrine was announced formally in a paper submitted to the US Congress on 20 September 2002. Declaring that the era of deterrence and containment was over, the paper committed the US – acting alone if necessary – to a far-reaching pre-emptive campaign against terrorism. At the same time, the paper includes a classical Wilsonian declaration of American universalism. American institutions are the only possible model for the world, it declares; the twentieth century ended with 'a decisive victory for the forces of freedom – and a single sustainable model for national success: freedom, democracy and free enterprise'.[4]

Pre-empting danger is a tempting strategy. It holds out the hope that the problems raised by terrorism are fully soluble. In truth, however, they are not.

Counter-terrorism is often linked with the 'war on drugs'. If they are alike, however, it is in the fact that neither campaign can be won.

Terrorism and the trade in illegal drugs are intertwined.[5] Most terrorist organisations derive a significant portion of their income from the drugs trade. In many parts of the world, they have formed symbiotic relationships with organised crime. Crimes such as trafficking in people and identity theft are part of their everyday business.

Terrorism and crime go together, but waging war on both fronts makes little sense. After vast expenditure and huge loss of liberty, the world still faces an illegal drugs pandemic. If the campaign against terrorism is modelled on the war against drugs, it is already lost.

Most of the worst evils of drugs can be removed by legalising them. Such a policy would have many benefits in terms of public health and crime control. More to the present point, it would strike a blow at one of the chief sources of income of terrorist groups. Unfortunately, except in a few European countries, legalising drugs is politically impossible.

While a policy of legalisation would eliminate the most damaging effects of illegal drugs, there is no similar remedy for terrorism. It can be deterred and subdued and its causes mitigated. It cannot be eradicated.

Consider the British case. Terrorist groups have been active in Northern Ireland and on the British mainland since the early 1970s. Several leading figures have been assassinated – Lord Mountbatten, a member of the royal family, was murdered while sailing his yacht; Airey Neave, a wartime escaper and the MP who organised the campaign in which Margaret Thatcher became leader of the Conservative Party, was assassinated within the House of Commons. Much of the British Cabinet was nearly taken out in an IRA attack on the Grand Hotel in Brighton during the Tory party conference in 1984 which killed five people and left over thirty seriously injured. Over the past thirty years, terrorist casualties in Britain have run into thousands.

The British government has used a variety of strategies to contain terrorism – military, political and diplomatic. There are some conditions working in its favour. It has a high level of control over Northern Ireland. Europe is a zone of peace. The governments of neighbouring states have been cooperative. Partly because of these factors, counter-terrorism has achieved some notable successes. Nevertheless, terrorism has not been eradicated.

The problems in dealing with Al Qaeda are vastly greater. It is based in territories all over the world. Over many of these the US has little or no control. Some are under strong pressure from Islamist movements. In some regions Al Qaeda has been able to exploit a popular sense of injustice. This is true in the Palestinian territories, in which it showed little interest for many years but where it has now succeeded in identifying itself with the *intifada*.

Unconventional warfare is rooted in deep-seated conflicts. The threat it poses is aggravated by the spread of weapons of mass destruction. Concerted action by many states can slow the process, as is shown by the partial success of efforts to restrain nuclear proliferation; but the leakage of dangerous technologies cannot be halted. In the end, it is a by-product of the diffusion of scientific knowledge.

Global conflict arises from the interaction of new technologies with age-old religious and ethnic divisions, a mix whose volatility is compounded by increased competition for natural resources. It is a combination made more explosive by the rash of failed states. Pre-emptive strikes against 'rogue states' cannot disable terrorist networks that take refuge in zones where states have collapsed. Where no government is in control of events, securing 'regime change' is futile. If pursued without the authority of institutions such as the UN, pre-emptive action will alienate other countries. It will thereby damage the international co-operation that is needed to contain terrorism. The US cannot be made safe from an intractably disordered world. By pursuing an illusion of impregnability it will only make itself more vulnerable.

American plans for regime change evoke suspicion and hostility in many countries. A year after Al Qaeda's attacks, America was more widely resented than it had ever been. This is the third obstacle to Pax Americana.

In the medium term, the Bush administration's belief in 'a single sustainable model' of human development could prove more dangerous than the strategy of pre-empting threats. Exporting American institutions makes sense only on the premise that at bottom everyone shares American values. That could prove a costly conceit.

In any realistic scenario, the US will have to learn to live with states that have no wish to share its values. After all, they include nearly all the states in the world. Strategically allied in the Cold War and – already less convincingly – during the post-Cold War period, Europe and America are reverting to being the alien civilisations they were before the First World War. In Asia, the claim that the US embodies the only sustainable model of human development is viewed with incredulity, if not contempt.

This resistance to American attempts to impose a single model on the rest of the world adds an extra layer of risk to the strategy of pre-empting threats. American military intervention in a region such as the Middle East has a reasonable prospect of success when – as in the Gulf War – its goals are limited. When it seeks to engineer political changes it risks a dangerous blowback. The destabilising impact could extend to countries as distant as Pakistan, Indonesia and the Philippines. Pursuing regime changes in the Middle East will effect a revolutionary unsettlement in the region not unlike that which was produced by President Woodrow Wilson's attempt to implement national self-determination in Central and Eastern Europe after the First World War. Now, as then, the result of seeking to export American values is likely to be chaos.

US policy today differs in some ways from that of the Wilsonian era. In promoting nationalism in Central and Eastern Europe Wilson was exporting an American version of a European doctrine into parts of Europe where it could only foment upheaval. Nationalism in Eastern Europe and the Balkans has rarely been of the civic variety that unified countries such as France and Italy. Usually it has a strong ethnic component – a dangerously divisive factor in regions where populations are mixed and borders disputed. Even the wisest policies could not have preserved Europe from instability after the First World War; but the effect of Wilson's intervention was to make large-scale upheaval a certainty.

There is another difference. Woodrow Wilson's attempt to reshape Europe was fundamentally an Enlightenment project. The world it envisaged was one that would be easily recognised by Mazzini, Garibaldi and other liberal European nationalists. At the start of the twenty-first century, American universalism has a more apocalyptic flavour. In some degree this reflects contingencies of US politics. The Republican Party owes a great deal – not least in terms of funding – to fundamentalist Christian groups. Part of the drive to reshape the Middle East comes from the Christian fundamentalist belief that a major conflagration will fulfil biblical prophecies of a catastrophic conflict in the region. To the extent that it reflects this type of thinking, American foreign policy is itself fundamentalist.

If there is any coherent argument animating America's revolutionary foreign policies, it is that 'market states' are now the only legitimate mode of government.[6] In this view, global capital markets and a universal culture of human rights are killing off the nation-state. The only kind of regime that can claim legitimacy is a market state, which aims simply to facilitate prosperity for its citizens.

Undeniably, prosperity is now one of the requirements of legitimate government.[7] That does not mean it is the only requirement, or always the most important. Modern states exist to meet enduring human needs, among which security from violence and recognition of cultural identity are as important as they have ever been. No state that fails to meet these needs is likely to survive for long.

States that meet these needs need not be nation-states. A neo-imperial regime such as Putin's Russia may achieve legitimacy by embodying an historic sense of identity – largely but not exclusively Russian – that distinguishes its citizens from 'the West', and by providing security against disorder. A city-state such as Singapore can do the same. Popularly legitimate states need not be democracies. Where a move to democracy might involve weakening government, an authoritarian regime is often seen as more legitimate. Plausibly, this was the case in China after the events in Tiananmen Square.

Nor does a state need to promote prosperity to be accepted as legitimate. Prosperity is not so much a requirement of legitimate government as one of its consequences. Where vital human needs for security or recognition are not met, rising incomes yield political instability. As Alexis de Tocqueville observed, the French *ancien régime* was overthrown because the condition of the people had recently improved.

Today, as in the past, fear is more potent in politics than hope of gain. The mass of humanity cares more about security than it does about prosperity. States that deliver safety are more legitimate than those that promise wealth.

Market states are phantoms, not historical realities. Where they have a semblance of existence – as in the United States – it is because the particular cultural identities they express have been screened from view. The market state is a singularly American construction, which cannot be established in any other country. To seek to implant it in the Arab world is particularly hazardous.

Arab regimes come in many varieties, but few of them have deep popular legitimacy. Saudi Arabia is a post-imperial construction tilting unsteadily towards anti-western theocracy. Iraq is also a creation of departing imperialists, but the regime of Saddam Hussein is an essentially western state whose closest affinities are with the former Soviet Union.

Whatever their differences, few Arab regimes have ever been functioning democracies. That does not mean American attempts to export democracy will be welcomed. Neither the hyper-subtle Arab élites nor the masses in the streets accept that there is only 'one sustainable model' of development. In a region where American power is implacably hated, indigenous Arab tyrannies are more likely to be accepted as legitimate than American-backed 'market states'.

Far from ushering in a new era of global governance, globalisation is producing a rebirth of empire. Imperial governance is being quietly reinvented as the only remedy for the dangers that flow from failed states; but the protectorates that have been established so far – in countries such as Bosnia, Kosovo and Afghanistan – are not simple projections of American power. They are international enterprises, working within the framework of institutions such as NATO, the EU and the UN. In a time when US power is widely resented, such ventures have a better prospect of survival than any purely American construction. A new type of imperial governance is emerging, defensive and cooperative rather than expansionist in its aims.[8]

If there is danger in this new imperialism, it is that the advanced industrial countries will lose interest. The US in particular shows little readiness for the long haul of state building. Except where scarce natural resources are at stake, countries governed by international protectorates are more likely to face abandonment than a new form of colonial exploitation. The likelihood is that neo-imperialism will be a last resort, taken up in crisis and given up at leisure.

This is not to say that crises will be uncommon. Al Qaeda is unlikely to be at the centre of resistance to US power for more than a decade or so. Radical Islam is likely to be only the first of a number of challenges to American hegemony. Asymmetric warfare will undoubtedly continue, with new protagonists we cannot foresee. Sooner or later the emerging powers of Asia will seek to remould an international system shaped by American power.

By the middle of the present century China may be in a position to challenge American hegemony. Certainly that looks to be the working assumption of American military planners, who appear to be shaping US conventional forces with such an eventuality in mind. It would be foolish to discount as unrealistic the possibility of war between these two great powers.

The medium-term prospects of the US retaining its position as the sole mega-power are not notably favourable. New technology is being disseminated at increasing speed. Presently unchallengeable, America's military superiority will be eroded by the very processes of globalisation whose virtues the US has recently lauded. With industrialisation advancing rapidly, the acquisition of high-tech weapons systems will soon follow. America's global hegemony may prove as fleeting as Britain's – if not more so.

In the last analysis, the world will not accept a Pax Americana because it resists the imposition of American values. For many Americans, this may seem paradoxical. Are not American ideals shared by all of humankind? The answer is that insofar as they are American, they are not. Beyond its shores, no one accepts America's claim to be the model for a universal civilisation.

Fifty years ago, George Santayana wrote about the prospect of an American empire:

The authority that controlled universal economy, if it were in American hands, would irresistibly tend to control education and training also. It might set up, as was done in the American zone in Germany, a cultural department, with ideological and political propaganda. The philanthropic passion for service would prompt social, if not legal intervention in the traditional life of all other nations, not only by selling there innumerable American products, but by recommending, if not imposing, American ways of living and thinking.[9]

Americans see their country as embodying universal values. Other countries see the American way of life as one among many; they do not believe it ever will – or should – be universal. Knowing from long experience how easily friends and enemies change places, they resist the division of the world into 'good' and 'evil' regimes. Perceiving the US as a proselytising regime, they fear its interventions. They prefer the dangers of a world without a hegemonic power to a world made over in an American image.

Americans will support a Pax Americana only if it promotes values that they believe to be shared by all humanity; but it is just such a peace that the majority of mankind will find most oppressive. In the volatile mix of geopolitical calculation and messianic enthusiasm that is presently shaping America's foreign policy, it is not American *realpolitik* that the world most resents. It is American universalism.

8

Why we still do not know
what it means to be modern

That history just unfolds, independently of a specified direction,
of a goal, no one is willing to admit.

E. M. Cioran[1]

The word 'modern' appeared first in English towards the
end of the sixteenth century. To begin with it meant little
more than being of the present time, but slowly it came to
carry a sense of novelty. 'Modern' meant something that
had never existed before. The idea was conceived that the
future would be different from the past.

This idea was itself new. The Greeks and the Romans
believed that history was a series of cycles; the future was
a rerun of the past. Medieval Europeans saw history differently, as a moral drama that concluded with the end of the
world; but they never doubted that the conditions of
earthly life would remain much as they had always been. If
they imagined a world in which humans lived differently,
they situated it not in the future but in far-off places that
had not yet been mapped.

This practice continued well into the eighteenth century. Samuel Johnson's *Rasselas* (1759) describes different
modes of human life through the fiction of long voyages to
unknown lands.[2] Johnson's Abyssinian Prince Rasselas

leaves the Happy Valley of his birth to wander in search of the best way of living. It did not occur to Johnson to set his tale in the future. The future had not yet been invented.

By the end of the eighteenth century, the future had become the site of a better world. 'Modern' meant something benign – an irreversible historical condition in which knowledge, wealth and human happiness were increasing together. It was this condition that Edward Gibbon described when he wrote in 1776:

It may be safely presumed that no people, unless the face of nature is changed, will relapse into their original barbarism . . . We may therefore acquiesce in the pleasing conclusion that every age of the world has increased, and still increases, the real wealth, the happiness, the knowledge, and perhaps the virtue of the human race.'[3]

Gibbon was too good an historian to imagine that human life would ever be perfect; but he was enough of a man of his time to believe that it was much improved, and would in future be better than it had ever been. Neither Gibbon nor most other Enlightenment thinkers believed that progress was inevitable. They knew that history contained long detours and sudden reverses. Some even allowed that if the growth of knowledge faltered humanity could revert to barbarism.

What none of these thinkers doubted was that the advance of knowledge would be matched by a parallel convergence in ethics and politics. With the Positivists, this became the belief that science was the foundation of a universal civilisation – a belief accepted by nearly everyone today.

The trouble with this belief is not that it is a myth but that it is harmful. Human life could scarcely go on without myths. Certainly politics cannot. The flaw in the modern myth is that it tethers us to a hope of unity, when we should be learning to live with conflict.

In calling this a myth, the aim is to mark its origins in religion. The prevailing idea of what it means to be modern is a post-Christian myth. Christians have always held that that there is only one path to salvation, that it is disclosed in history and that it is open to all. In these respects, Christianity differs radically from the religions and philosophies of the ancient world and from non-western faiths.

In the polytheistic cults of the Greeks and Romans, it was accepted that humans will always live different ways. Where there are many gods no way of life is binding on all. Worshipping one god, Christians have always believed that only one way of life can be right.

In the ancient European mystery religions and in non-western faiths, history is known to be without meaning; salvation is understood as liberation from time. In interpreting history in terms of the salvation of the species, Christianity's only rival is Islam, which by virtue of the militant universalism it has displayed throughout much of its history belongs in 'the West'. Judaism is also an historical religion, but the history with which it is concerned is that of the Jews, not humanity as a whole. By making few universal claims Judaism has avoided the intolerance displayed by other monotheistic faiths.

Before Christianity, the idea that salvation is open to all

was unknown in the ancient world. The classical philosophers – Plato and Aristotle, the Stoics and the Epicureans – took for granted that no more than a few would ever live the good life. In mystery religions such as Mithraism, only an élite of initiates could hope for salvation.

Enlightenment thinkers like to see themselves as modern pagans, but they are really latter-day Christians: they too aim to save mankind. The ancient pagans did not believe that the mass of mankind could be saved. Or, for that matter, that it was worth saving.

Believing that one way of life is best for all of mankind and viewing history as the struggle to achieve it, Marxism and neo-liberalism are post-Christian cults. Beyond Christendom, no one has ever imagined that 'world communism' or 'global capitalism' could be 'the end of history'. The Positivists believed that with the advance of knowledge humanity would come to share the same values; but this is because they had inherited from Christianity the belief that history is working to a finale in which all are saved. Take away this residue of faith, and you will see that while science makes progress, humanity does not.

If we strip away from Positivism the eschatological hopes it inherited from Christianity, what remains is not far from the truth. St-Simon and Comte believed that technology is the driving force of history. In this they were right. History is a series of accidents; but if it has any discernible trend it is the growing power of human invention. What we commonly call the modern period is only a quickening of this process.

Despite their protestations, the Positivists' view of history owed little to science. Like Christianity, it was an historical teleology – a narrative of the advance of humanity to a pre-ordained goal. As Stuart Hampshire has written: 'The Positivists believed that all societies across the globe will gradually discard their traditional attachments . . . because of the need for rational, scientific and experimental modes of thought which a modern industrial economy involves. This is an old faith, widespread in the nineteenth century, that there must be a step-by-step convergence on liberal values, on "our values" . . . We now know there is no "must" about it and that such theories have a predictive value of zero.'[4]

Positivism is a doctrine of redemption in the guise of a theory of history. The Positivists inherited the Christian view of history, but – suppressing Christianity's saving insight that human nature is ineradicably flawed – they announced that by the use of technology humanity could make a new world. When they suggested that in the third and final stage of history there would be no politics, only rational administration, they imagined they were being scientific; but the belief that science can enable humanity to transcend its historic conflicts and create a universal civilisation is not a product of empirical inquiry. It is a remnant of monotheism.

The Positivist vision of the future has another source in religion. Christians believe the Earth has been given to mankind to meet its needs. Saint-Simon and Comte believed this too, but they stated it in the terms of science: the planet is a heap of resources available for human use. What Comte called an industrial society – industrialism being another of the terms he coined – is dedicated to the satisfaction of human wants through the efficient exploitation of these resources. When all societies have become industrial the three stages of history will be complete.

In this Positivist view of things, humans are productive animals, whose lives are fulfilled in labour. An industrial society enables them to exploit the natural resources of the planet. By doing so, they can conquer material scarcity. A new science of society will be developed, in which intractable questions of ethics become matters of expert judgement. With scarcity overcome and ethics a science, the causes of human conflict will be eliminated.

We laugh at the enthusiasm of these prophets of modernity for the pseudo-science of phrenology. Yet free market economics is no different. Like its predecessor, 'scientific socialism', it rests on a spurious claim to knowledge of the future.

Contemporary social scientists have followed Saint-Simon and Comte in believing that social science can establish universal laws of human behaviour, and thereby forecast the future development of mankind. Unfortunately – from the point of view of the project of a science of society – the behaviour of human beings cannot be predicted in this way. As Alasdair MacIntyre has written: 'the salient fact about those [social] sciences is the absence of the discovery of any law-like generalisations whatsoever . . . No economist predicted "stagflation" before it occurred; the writings of monetary economists have signally failed to predict the rates of inflation correctly.'[5]

The science of society of which Saint-Simon and Comte dreamt is nowhere in sight. The reason is not that the Positivists were premature or over-ambitious. Their view of science was unscientific.

For the Positivists, the advance of science is a sign of the progress of the human mind. In fact, as we know it today, science is an accident of history. Over the past two thousand years or so, many cultures have displayed an interest in technology; many have engaged in natural philosophy and cosmological speculation. No single culture can claim credit for the rapid development of science in recent centuries.

The rise of science to its present ascendancy is the result of a highly adventitious mix of influences. It is sometimes asked why science did not develop further in China, which in terms of technology was for many centuries far ahead of any European country. If we understand the contingency of science the question does not arise. A great twentieth-century Sinologist has written:

It must be taken for granted that in China concern for the practically useful stimulated causal thinking in technology as strongly as in the West, and contributed as much or more to material well-being until it was outstripped in the last few centuries. But to assume that this would be bringing China nearer to modern science assumes an obsolete conception of science as developing by continuous progress in rationality. We now think in terms of a Scientific Revolution about AD 1600, the 'discovery of how to discover', the quite sudden integration of the idea of explaining all natural phenomena by mathematised laws testable by controlled experiment . . . The Scientific Revolution appears as a unique and complex event, depending on a variety of social and other conditions, including a confluence of discoveries (Greek, Indian, Chinese, Arabic, scarcely ever Roman) centred on the combining of Indian numerals and algebra with Greek logic and geometry. Since this crucial combination, for primarily geographical reasons, came about among the Arabs, afterwards passing to Latin Christendom, it becomes pointless to ask why the Scientific Revolution did not happen in some other part of the world.[6]

The rise of science was not inevitable. There are many plausible historical scenarios in which it need never have happened; but once it did it engendered the world in which we live today. At bottom, the modern world is a jumble of things engendered by the accelerating advance of knowledge. The spread of literacy and the growth of cities, the expansion of trade and the spread of industry – all these trends are by-products of expanding scientific knowledge. None works to promote any particular values.

If science drives history, it does not do so in any particular direction, or in conformity with any purpose. Racial domination and better education, increased longevity and genocide – these are only a few of the many divergent goals that science has served. History shows that human beings use their growing knowledge to advance the purposes they already have – however conflicting they may be.

That humans are bound to use science in this way is shown by science itself. Darwin teaches that 'humanity' is only an abstract term signifying a shifting current of genes. Humans are an animal species much like any other – more inventive and destructive, no doubt, but like other animals in using their resources to survive and reproduce.

108

Contemporary Darwinians are adamant that Darwin's discovery leaves the future in human hands. Other species may be ruled by natural selection, but we are not. What humanity does with scientific knowledge is 'up to us'. If Darwinism is true, this must be false. 'We' are few, feeble and animals like the rest.

As with any part of science, the Darwinian worldview cannot be taken as the final truth. Contrary to the Positivists and their disciples in the Vienna School, there is nothing to say that science is bound to yield a single view of the world: 'science contains many different and yet empirically acceptable worldviews, each one containing its own metaphysical background.'[7] Science surely rules out some worldviews, such as those required by phrenology or Nazi 'racial science'; but it is only a metaphysical faith in the uniformity of Nature that supports the idea that one day a single view of things will be left alone in the field.

Still, Darwinism is one of the strongest strands in contemporary science, and it teaches that the human mind evolved for reproductive success. There is no room in this theory for free will – a notion that comes from religion, not science. True, we are not bound to seek survival and reproduction in all that we do; but if we stray too far from their imperatives we will leave no descendants. Science cannot avoid serving the human animal's actual needs.

In the modern myth, science is a type of gnosis, a higher form of knowledge through which humanity can resolve dilemmas that throughout its history have resisted any solution. Looked at through the lens of science itself, science is a tool devised by a highly inventive animal to exploit its environment. It cannot dispel mystery, or conjure away tragedy. As Wittgenstein wrote: 'When all possible scientific questions have been answered, the problems of life remain completely untouched.'[8]

The belief that scientific advance engenders social progress suggests that science and ethics are alike, when in fact they are very different. Once it has been acquired and disseminated, scientific knowledge cannot now be lost; but there is no ethical or political advance that cannot be reversed. In science, the approach to truth is an unmixed good; but in ethics and politics there are no unmixed goods. Science is a cumulative activity. Human life is not.

There may be some types of society in which science cannot flourish, but there is no one type that it advances. Any society that has the power of invention is modern. Not all societies can be modern. That does not mean that only one kind can be.

Many societies have done without science for long periods. The Tasmanian aboriginals did not aim to control their environment. Rather, through myth and magic, they aimed to live in harmony with it. Following this path, they survived and renewed their culture for many generations. Yet they were defenceless when confronted with more technologically advanced European settlers. Their genocide is only an extreme version of the fate of hunter-gatherer peoples everywhere.[9]

In a predatory world, peoples that lack the power of invention go to the wall; but there is no one kind of society that possesses that power. Science flourishes in many cultures and regimes, and so does technology. Theocratic and totalitarian regimes are inhospitable to science, but that is far from saying that it thrives only in liberal societies.

For a society to be genuinely modern, it must have the capacity to generate new knowledge, and not merely use knowledge that has been acquired by others. Some societies survive by borrowing or stealing technology. Between the eighteenth and twentieth centuries, the life of the American Plains Indians was based on tools – such as guns – they could neither make nor even repair. The Taliban were capable of using advanced technology they bought or stole; but it is unlikely that they could ever have developed it. Had it survived for a generation or more, Nazi Germany might have fallen back in scientific research through having driven many of the best scientists abroad. Even the former Soviet Union owed much of its technology to borrowings from other sources.

The belief that liberal societies are uniquely favourable to science comes from a narrow view of history. Before the First World War, Imperial Germany was a successful example of authoritarian modernisation, displaying an impressive rate of technical advance. Much the same was true in Tsarist Russia. The failure of these regimes was not inevitable. They were casualties of the fortunes of war. It was not any inherent affinity of science with liberal values, but Cleopatra's nose – the role of accident in history – that destroyed them.

History suggests that science will continue to flourish far beyond the confines of liberal values. As we have seen, its rise is a result of Arab, Indian and Chinese influences, among others. If these and other cultures are sites of scientific advance in the future, it is likely to be in regimes that owe little to western models.

The Positivists believed that modern societies would be the same everywhere. Most people believe the same today. The truth is that we cannot know in advance what it means to be modern. If the modern period is simply the mix of things produced by accelerating scientific advance, modern societies will vary widely and unpredictably.

This is the true meaning of globalisation. In the sense in which it is used by politicians, it refers to the global free market that was constructed at the end of the Cold War, but it really signifies no more than the widening and deepening connections that are being created throughout the world by new information and communication technologies that abolish or foreshorten time and distance. In the popular mind, the latter works to strengthen the former. In fact, a contrary process is at work.

As a technological development, globalisation began with the laying down of underwater transatlantic telegraph cables in the second half of the nineteenth century, and has continued despite the Great Depression, two world wars and the rise and fall of communism.[10] The global free market is a political construction not much more than a dozen years old. Technological globalisation is an inexorable process, which no political decision can halt. When the two collide, it is obvious which will win.

Globalisation begets de-globalisation. By intensifying competition for natural resources and hastening the spread of weapons of mass destruction, the dissemination of new technology throughout the world magnifies some of the most dangerous human conflicts. Neo-liberal utopians expected that globalisation would fill the world with liberal republics, linked together in peace and trade. History is responding with a flowering of war, tyranny and empire.

As societies throughout the world become more modern, they do *not* thereby become more similar. Often they move further apart. In these circumstances, we need to think afresh about how regimes and ways of life that will always be different can come to coexist in peace.

Rather than looking to an illusive future we would do better to turn to the past. Toleration was practised many centuries ago in Buddhist India, in the Ottoman Empire and the Moorish kingdoms of medieval Spain, and in China. There is nothing peculiarly liberal, western or modern about the peaceful coexistence of communities having different values and beliefs.

Such regimes cannot simply be reinvented. They were devices for peaceful coexistence in times when most people were born into a single way of life. Today, many societies harbour many ways of life, with many people belonging to more than one. Even so, these ancient regimes of toleration teach a vital lesson. Liberal societies are only one way in which different ways of life can live together.

The modern myth is that with the advance of science one set of values will be accepted everywhere. Can we not accept that human beings have divergent and conflicting values, and learn to live with this fact? It is a strange notion that humanity is destined for a single way of living, when history is so rich in conflict and contrivance.

In the recent past, a diversity of regimes and economic systems was taken as given. Throughout most of the modern period, few practising politicians took seriously the idea that a single regime could encompass all of humankind. It was only after the First World War, when secular ideology seized control of government, that politics and war became missions to save mankind.

We can imagine a future in which each country would be free to find its own version of modernity. If a country wished to limit its contacts with the rest of the world, it would be left in peace. Societies with widely diverging histories and values would be allowed to develop correspondingly divergent economic systems. If countries sought to establish alternative monetary systems, they would be free to do so. Projects such as Islamic banking may not be fully practicable; but they can hardly be as unrealistic as the madcap schemes imposed on many countries by the IMF and the World Bank. In a world containing many regimes and several economic systems, international institutions would be charged with framing minimum terms of peaceful coexistence. Trade agreements would be made bilaterally on terms agreeable to the countries (or associations of countries) concerned. Unless a regime was a demonstrable threat to peace, no attempt would be made to induce it to alter its form of government. Even intolerable regimes would be tolerated so long as they posed no danger to others.

Though we can imagine such a world, it is hard to imagine anything resembling it coming about by design. The proselytising fury of faith – religious and secular – forbids any peaceful evolution. The normal diversity of regimes will return, but not before the world has endured great upheaval.

Without a doubt, a more fragmented world would be a safer world. It would still be at risk of horrifying violence. There cannot be tolerance so long as terrorism is unchecked. Dealing with it is a precondition of any kind of civilised existence, and requires courage, skill and – at times – ruthlessness. Yet in the new kind of unconventional war that is now being fought there is no prospect of victory.

Given the scale of the conflicts engendered by the quickening advance of science, what is most needed is not the perpetual ranting uplift of secular hope. It is the willingness to act resolutely without the hope of any final success. Rather than seeking solutions for the dilemmas created by the advance of knowledge, we should accept them as framing the world in which we must live.

The conflicts that wrack the world today would not have surprised the pagans of classical antiquity. For them, no 'indissoluble chain' bound knowledge, virtue and happiness together. In the plays of Euripides, knowledge cannot undo the workings of fate; virtue gives no protection against disaster. The most that humans can do is to be brave and resourceful, and expect to achieve little. Very likely we cannot revive this pagan view of things; but perhaps we can learn from it how to limit our hopes.[11]

The dangers arising from the growth of knowledge are not problems that can be solved. They are evils to be staved off from day to day. Science cannot rid us of the conflicts of ethics and politics. Tyranny is bad, but so is anarchy. The state is necessary to protect us against violence, but it easily turns violent itself. We must contain terrorism if we are to have any kind of civilised life, but in doing so we run the risk of compromising the life we are trying to protect. Such conflicts are normal.

In contemporary western societies, repressed religion returns in secular cults. When Saint-Simon and Comte founded the Religion of Humanity they devised the prototype of every subsequent political religion. The eschatological hopes that animated these intermittently sane nineteenth-century savants shaped Marxian 'scientific socialism' and neo-liberal 'free-market economics'. In dilute and timorous form, they sustain liberal humanists today. Repressed from conscious awareness, the apocalyptic passions of religion have returned as projects of universal human emancipation.

With only a little hyperbole, one might define secular culture in terms of this Freudian cycle. The mark of repressed thought and emotion is that it is shut away from conscious scrutiny. This is nowhere more evident than in the encounter of western societies with radical Islam. Western thinkers rightly note that Islam has never grasped the need for a secular realm. They fail to note that what passes for secular belief in the West is a mutation of religious faith.

The conflict between Al Qaeda and the West is a war of religion. The Enlightenment idea of a universal civilisation, which the West upholds against radical Islam, is an offspring of Christianity. Al Qaeda's peculiar hybrid of theocracy and anarchy is a by-product of western radical thought. Each of the protagonists in the current conflict is driven by beliefs that are opaque to it.

The chiliastic violence of radical Islam is not the product of any 'clash of civilisations'. The twentieth century's grand experiments in revolutionary terror were not assaults on the West. They expressed ambitions that have been harboured only in the West.

The death camps of Nazi Germany and the gulags of Soviet Russia and Maoist China killed many millions of people, far more than in any earlier century. Yet it is not the number of the dead that is peculiarly modern. It is the belief that as a result of these deaths a new world would be born. In former times, the Inquisition tortured and killed on a large scale; but it did not imagine it would remake the world through terror. It promised salvation in the world hereafter, not paradise in the world below. In contrast, in the twentieth century, industrial-scale killing by states of their own citizens has been practised in the belief that the survivors will live in a world better than any that has ever existed.

As has truly been written:

To destroy a city, a state, an empire even, is an essentially finite act; but to attempt the total annihilation – the liquidation – of so ubiquitous but so theoretically or ideologically defined an entity as a social class or racial abstraction is quite another, and one impossible even in conception to a mind not conditioned by Western habits of thought. Here is a truly Faustian ambition – to

117

transform by physical action not merely the earth, but the qualities of the creatures who dwell upon it, an ambition related to the modern quest for the breaking down of mountains, the escape from the bounds of the earth, the control and reform of human genetics, the manipulation of life itself – all of them ambitions which, before this century, were the dark matter of myth and necromancy. Yet such have been the stated ambitions of the two political movements, Communism and Fascism, which have convulsed the middle years of our century.[12]

Self-evidently, the belief that terror can remake the world is not a result of any kind of scientific inquiry. It is faith, pure and simple. No less incontrovertibly, the faith is uniquely western.

Western societies are ruled by the myth that, as the rest of the world absorbs science and becomes modern, it is bound to become secular, enlightened and peaceful – as, contrary to all evidence, they imagine themselves to be. With its attack on the Twin Towers, Al Qaeda destroyed this myth; and yet it continues to be believed. Al Qaeda is driven by the belief that the world can be transformed by spectacular acts of terror. This myth has also been repeatedly disproved; but still it persists.

Myths are not refuted. They simply disappear, as the ways of life from which they sprang fade from the world. Science teaches limits, but intermingled with eschatological myths it has kindled limitless ambitions. The result is the unbounded violence of modern times, which Al Qaeda continues. It is not the first attempt to remake the world by terror, and it will not be the last. Once Al Qaeda has disappeared, other types of terror – very likely not animated by radical Islam, possibly not overtly religious – will surely follow. The advance of knowledge does not portend any age of reason. It merely adds another twist to human folly.

In a flash of clairvoyance, Henri Saint-Simon speculated that the future of mankind might lie in a meeting of Voltaire and de Maistre. The exemplary Enlightenment *philosophe* and the incomparable reactionary are an odd couple. Cold logic fused with incurable irrationality makes a curious prospect. Yet it is the interaction of expanding scientific knowledge with unchanging human needs that will determine the future of the species.

The human prospect is shaped by rising human numbers, mounting competition for natural resources and the spread of weapons of mass destruction. Each of these forces is a by-product of the growth of scientific knowledge. Interacting with historic ethnic and religious enmities, they augur conflicts as destructive as any in the twentieth century.

By enlarging human power, science has generated the illusion that humanity can take charge of its destiny. Borne along on a flood of invention, the modern world believes it has left the past behind. Instead, taken up by human beings to serve their needs and illusions, science continues the drift of history.

References

Introduction

1 A year before the war, in March 2002, I warned that 'toppling Saddam might lead to the fragmentation of the Iraqi state', while on the eve of war in March 2003 I pointed to the risk that 'the Iraqi state, a rickety structure cobbled together by departing British civil servants, will fracture and fragment in Yugoslav or even Chechen fashion'. See John Gray, *Heresies: Against Progress and Other Illusions*, London: Granta Books, 2004, pp.98, 140.

2 Francis Fukuyama – himself an erstwhile neo-conservative – has noted the Leninist character of neo-conservative foreign policy in his book, *After the Neo-Cons: America at the Crossroads*, London: Profile Books, 2006, pp.54–5.

3 For a probing analysis of the ways in which the United States has used radical Islamist movements to further its foreign policy objectives, see Robert Dreyfuss, *Devil's Game: How the US Helped Unleash Fundamentalist Islam*, New York: Henry Holt/Metropolitan Books, 2005.

4 Olivier Roy, *Globalised Islam: The Search for a New Ummah*, London: Hurst and Company, 2004, p.25.

5 Robert Pape provides an illuminating examination of the origins and purposes of suicide bombing in a number of different historical contexts in *Dying to Win: The Strategic Logic of Suicide Bombing*, Random House: New York, 2005.

6 Norman Cohn, *The Pursuit of the Millennium: Revolutionary Millenarians and Mystical Anarchists of the Middle Ages*, Oxford and New York; Oxford University Press, 1972.

1 What Al Qaeda destroyed

1 Alexander Herzen, *My Past and Thoughts*, Berkeley, Los Angeles and London: University of California Press, 1999, p.523.

2 Three modern projects

1 Paul Valery, *Collected Works*, vol. 10, *History and Politics*, New York: Pantheon, Bollingen Series, 1962, p.28.
2 For a seminal interpretation of the Enlightenment belief in progress, see Carl L. Becker, *The Heavenly City of the Eighteenth Century Philosophers*, New Haven and London: Yale University Press, 1932. I have discussed the role of Enlightenment beliefs in modern political religions in *Enlightenment's Wake: Politics and Culture at the Close of the Modern Age*, London and New York: Routledge, 1995, Chapter 10, and *Endgames: Questions in Late Modern Political Thought*, Cambridge: Polity Press, 1997, Chapter 10.
3 On Voltaire's equivocations regarding progress, see my *Voltaire and Enlightenment*, London and New York: Phoenix/Orion and Routledge, 1999.
4 For an unsurpassed history of the Soviet experiment, see Michel Heller and Aleksander Nekrich, *Utopia in Power*, London: Hutchinson, 1985.
5 For one of the more interesting views of Nazism as an anti-western movement, see Aurel Kolnai's book, *The War Against the West*, London: Victor Gollancz, 1938.
6 Arthur Koestler, *Arrival and Departure*, London: Jonathan Cape, 1943, pp.142–4.
7 Herman Von Rauschning, *The Revolution of Nihilism: Warning to the West*, New York: Longman Green and Co., 1939, p.19.
8 For a fascinating account of the European experiment in moving beyond the modern nation-state, see Robert Cooper, *The Post-Modern State and the World Order*, London: Demos, 2nd edn, 2000.
9 I discuss Japanese modernisation in *False Dawn: Delusions of*

Global Capitalism, London and New York: Granta Books, 2002, pp.168–73.

10 Martin Woolf, *Financial Times*, 4 September 2002. A similar view of Al Qaeda is presented in Thomas L. Friedman, *Longitudes and Attitudes: Exploring the World After September 11*, New York: Farrar, Straus and Giroux, 2002.

11 For a magnificent study of late medieval and early modern millenarian movements, see Norman Cohn, *The Pursuit of the Millennium*, Oxford and New York: Oxford University Press, revised edn, 1970.

12 Joseph Conrad, *The Secret Agent: A Simple Tale*, 1907. The quotations come from the World's Classics Edition, Oxford and New York: Oxford University Press, 1983, pp.31–4.

13 These details are taken from Malise Ruthven's brilliant study, *A Fury for God: The Islamist Attack on America*, London and New York: Granta, 2002. The quotations can be found on pp.80, 81. For a valuable guide to the impact of radical Islam in Asia, see Ahmed Rashid, *Taliban: Militant Islam, Oil and Fundamentalism in Central Asia*, New Jersey: Yale University Press, 2002, and *Jihad: The Rise of Militant Islam in Central Asia*, New Jersey: Yale University Press, 2002. See also Fred Halliday, *Two Hours That Shook The World: September 11th, 2001, Causes and Consequences*, London: Saqui Books, 2002.

14 Malise Ruthven, *A Fury for God: The Islamist Attack on America*, p.91.

15 Leonard Binder, *Islamic Liberalism: A Critique of Development Ideologies*, Chicago, 1988, p.193. Binder is cited by Ruthven, op.cit., p.82.

16 For a discussion of the origins and development of the European Counter-Enlightenment, see 'The Counter-Enlightenment' in Isaiah Berlin, *Against the Current*, Oxford: Clarendon Press, 1991.

3 The original modernisers

1 L. Kolakowski, *Modernity on Endless Trial*, Chicago and London: University of Chicago Press, 1990, p.67.

2 For a thorough study of Saint-Simon, see Frank Manuel, *The New World of Henri Saint-Simon*, Cambridge, Mass.: Harvard University Press, 1956. Manuel presents a fascinating account of the leading Positivist savants and their milieu in his later book, *The Prophets of Paris*, Cambridge, Mass.: Harvard University Press, 1962.

3 Mary Pickering, *Auguste Comte: An Intellectual Biography*, vol. 1, Cambridge: Cambridge University Press, 1993, p.79.

4 *Henri Saint-Simon: Selected Writings on Science, Industry and Social Organisation*, ed. and trans. with an Introduction and Notes by Keith Taylor, London: Croom Helm, 1975, pp.78, 101.

5 Manuel, *The Prophets of Paris*, p.256.

6 The quote comes from Comte's French biographer Henri Gouhier, *La Jeunesse d'Auguste Comte*, Paris: Vrin, 1933–41, vol 1, p.146, and is quoted in Kenneth Thompson, *Auguste Comte: The Foundations of Sociology*, London: Nelson, 1976, p.9.

7 Manuel, *The Prophets of Paris*, p.265.

8 Auguste Comte, *The Catechism of Positive Religion*, trans. Richard Congreve, London: John Chapman, 1858, pp.303–4.

9 For John Stuart Mill's assessment of Comte, see Mill's interesting short book, *Auguste Comte and Positivism*, Ann Arbor: University of Michigan, 1973.

10 The quote from Condorcet comes from Emma Rothschild, *Economic Sentiments: Adam Smith, Condorcet and the Enlightenment*, Cambridge, Mass., and London: Harvard University Press, 2001, p.203. Rothschild's book contains a brilliant reinterpretation of Condorcet's thought.

11 *Henri Saint-Simon*, p.124.

12 Kenneth Thompson, *Auguste Comte: The Foundations of Sociology*, London, Nelson, 1976, p.44.

13 *Henri Saint-Simon*, p.123.

14 Thompson, *Auguste Comte*, p.43.

15 Ibid, p.58.

16 *Collected Writings of John Maynard Keynes*, vol. VII: *The General Theory of Employment, Interest and Money*, London: Macmillan/St Martin's Press, 1973, p.383.

4 A very short history of the global free market

1 John Lukacs, *At the End of an Age*, New Haven and London: Yale University Press, 2002, p.42.
2 Fukuyama announced the end of history in an article with that title in the summer 1989 issue of *National Interest*. In an essay on Fukuyama's article which I published in *National Review* on 27 October 1989, I wrote: 'Ours is an era in which political ideology, liberal as much as Marxist, has a dwindling leverage on events, and more ancient, more primordial forces, nationalist and religious, fundamentalist and soon, perhaps, Malthusian, are contesting with each other . . . If the Soviet Union does indeed fall apart, that beneficent catastrophe will not inaugurate a new era of post-historical harmony, but instead a return to the classical terrain of history, a terrain of great-power rivalries, secret diplomacies, and irredentist claims and wars.' See my article 'The End of History – or the end of liberalism?' in John Gray, *Post-liberalism: Studies in Political Thought*, London and New York: Routledge, 1993, p.249. For Michael Hardt's version of the view of America as the terminus of history, see Michael Hardt and Antonio Negri, *Empire*, Cambridge, Mass., and London: Harvard University Press, 2001.
3 For a brief consideration of the achievements of late Tsarism, see my paper, 'Totalitarianism, reform and civil society' in John Gray, *Post-liberalism: Studies in Political Thought*, pp.165–8.
4 I discuss Russian anarcho-capitalism in *False Dawn: Delusions of Global Capitalism*, London and New York: Granta Books and the New Press, 3rd edn with new foreword, 2002, pp.133–65. For a comprehensive account of market Bolshevism in Russia, see Peter Reddaway and Dmitri Glinski, *The Tragedy of Russia's Reforms: Market Bolshevism against Democracy*, Washington, DC: US Institute of Peace Press, 2001. For an authoritative and devastating critique of IMF policies in Russia, see Joseph Stiglitz, *Globalisation and Its Discontents*, London: Allen Lane/Penguin, 2002, Chapter 5.

See also Alexander Chubarov, *Russia's Bitter Path to Modernity: A History of the Soviet and Post-Soviet Eras*, New York and London: Continuum Books, 2001, and Robert Service, *Russia: Experiment with a People*, London: Macmillan, 2002.

5 I discuss some of the ironies of Russian modernisation in my book *Straw Dogs: Thoughts on Humans and Other Animals*, London and New York: Granta Books, 2002, pp.178–9.

6 See Joseph Stiglitz, 'Argentina Short-Changed: Why the Nation that Followed the Rules Fell to Pieces', *Washington Post*, 12 May 2002.

7 Herbert Croly, *The Promise of American Life*, Boston, Mass.: Northeastern University Press, 1989 (1909).

8 For a useful study of the religious dimension of economics in America, see Robert H. Nelson, *Economics as Religion: From Samuelson to Chicago and Beyond*, University Park Pennsylvania: Penn State University Press, 2001.

9 For a canonical statement of the triumphalist view of the American economy in the late Nineties, see Daniel Yergin, *The Commanding Heights: The Battle Between Government and the Marketplace that is Remaking the Modern World*, New York: Simon and Schuster, 1998.

10 John Kay, 'A True and Fair View of Productivity', *Financial Times*, 27 March 2002.

11 See Hyman Minsky, *Stabilizing an Unstable Economy*, New Haven and London: Yale University Press, 1986; George Soros, *The Alchemy of Finance*, New York: Simon and Schuster, 1987, and *On Globalization*, New York: Public Affairs, 2002.

12 In December 1997 I wrote: 'When western free marketers crow over the economic difficulties of Asian countries they are showing themselves to be – not for the first time – myopic and hubristic . . . financial crisis in Asia does not augur the universal spread of free markets. Instead it may be the prelude to a global deflationary crisis, in which the United States itself recoils from the regime of free trade and deregulated markets it is currently seeking to impose in Asia and throughout

the world': 'Forget Tigers, Keep an Eye on China', *Guardian*,
17 December 1997.

13 For a survey of the damage done to American retirement
plans by the stock market collapse, see Edward N. Wolff,
*Retirement Insecurity: The Income Shortfalls Awaiting the
Soon-to-Retire*, Washington, DC: Economic Policy Institute,
2002.

14 For a discussion of the role of the Chairman of the Federal
Reserve Bank in failing to prick the American stock market
bubble, see Andrew Smithers and Stephen Wright, *Valuing
Wall Street*, New York and London: McGraw-Hill, 2000,
Chapter 32, 'The Economic Consequences of Alan Greenspan',
pp.339–43. For another discussion of the overvaluation of the
American stock market, see Robert J. Shiller, *Irrational
Exuberance*, Princeton, NJ: Princeton University Press, 2000.

15 For America's experiment in mass incarceration, see my
book, *False Dawn: The Delusions of Global Capitalism*,
pp.116–19.

16 Liah Greenfeld, *The Spirit of Capitalism: Nationalism and
Economic Growth*, Cambridge, Mass., and London: Harvard
University Press, 2001, p.6.

5 Geopolitics and the limits of growth

1 Thomas Hobbes, *Leviathan*, Oxford and New York: Oxford
University Press, 1996, p.230.

2 For Spencer's distinction between militant and industrial
societies, see Herbert Spencer, *The Principles of Ethics*, vol. 2,
Indianapolis: Liberty Classics, 1978, pp.209–15, and *The Man
Versus The State*, Indianapolis: Liberty Classics, 1982, pp.153–9.

3 For a seminal argument against perpetual growth, see Donella
H. Meadows, Dennis L. Meadows, J. Randers and W. W.
Behrens III, *The Limits to Growth*, New York: Universe Books,
1972. For a conventional economic response, see H. D. S. Cole
et al., *Models of Doom: A Critique of the Limits of Growth*, New
York: Universe Books, 1973. For a powerful conservative argument against unlimited growth, see Fred C. Ikle, 'Growth

Without End: Our Perpetual Growth Utopia', *National Review*, 7 March 1994. I developed an argument against perpetual growth in 'An Agenda for Green Conservatism' in John Gray, *Beyond the New Right: Markets, Government and the Common Environment*, London and New York: Routledge, 1993.

4 Michael T. Klare, *Resource Wars: The New Landscape of Global Conflict*, New York: Henry Holt and Company, 2001, p.162. For a discussion of water scarcity and its consequences, see Diane Raines Ward, *Water Wars: Drought, Flood, Folly and the Politics of Thirst*, Riverhead Books, 2002.

5 For an account of the demographic and ecological roots of the Rwandan tragedy, see E. O. Wilson, *Consilience: The Unity of Knowledge*, London: Abacus, 1998, pp.321–2. Some of the causes of Rwanda's conflicts lie in colonial times: see Mahmood Mamdami, *When Victims Become Killers: Colonialism, Nativism and Genocide in Rwanda*, London: James Curry, 2001.

6 Robert D. Kaplan, *Warrior Politics: Why Leadership Demands a Pagan Ethos*, New York: Random House, 2002, pp.93–4. For a useful discussion of Malthus, see Donald Winch, *Malthus*, Oxford and New York: Oxford University Press, 1987.

7 Engels allowed that overpopulation might someday be a problem, but believed it would be solved by communism. He failed to make clear in what the solution would consist.

8 Quoted by G. Binney, 'The Petro-Population Parallel', *Journal of the Optimum Population Trust*, vol. 2, no. 1, April 2002, p.8.

9 For a survey of population trends in the Gulf, see Anthony H. Cordesman, 'Demographics and the Coming Youth Explosion in the Gulf', published by the Center for Strategic and International Studies, Washington, DC, 1998.

10 For an account of the overall connection between petroleum use and population growth, see G. Binney, op.cit., and Walter Younquist, 'The Post-Petroleum Paradigm – and Population', *Population and Environment: A Journal of Interdisciplinary Studies*, vol. 20, no. 4, March 1999. See also C. J. Campbell, *The*

Coming Oil Crisis, Brentwood, Essex: Multi-Science Publishing Company and Petroconsultants S.A., no date, pp.159–60.

11 For the formative role of disease in history, see William McNeill, *Plagues and Peoples*, Harmondsworth: Penguin, 1979, and M. B. A. Oldstone, *Viruses, Plagues and History*, Oxford: Oxford Unversity Press, 1998.

12 According to the US Energy Information Administration, by 2020 China is projected to import 70 per cent of its oil and 50 per cent of its gas. See Richard Sokolsky, Angela Rabasca, C. R. Neu, *The Role of Southeast Asia in US Strategy Towards China*, Rand Document, 2000, p.22.

13 J. I. Guoxing, 'Energy Security: A View From China', *PacNet* no. 25, 25 June 1999.

14 For a fascinating exploration of the impact of entropy on economic life, see Nicholas Georgescu-Roegen, *The Entropy Law and the Economic Process*, Cambridge, Mass., and London: Harvard University Press, 1971.

15 For an authoritative discussion of oil depletion by a geologist with long experience of the oil industry, see Kenneth S. Deffeyes, *Hubbert's Peak: The Impending World Oil Shortage*, Princeton and Oxford: Princeton University Press, 2001.

16 For an authoritative discussion of global warming, see James Lovelock, *Gaia: The Practical Science of Planetary Medicine*, London: Gaia Books, 2000.

6 The metamorphosis of war

1 Joseph de Maistre, *Considerations on France*, Cambridge: Cambridge University Press, 1994, p.27.

2 On the origins of modern war, see Martin van Creveld's brilliant book, *On Future War*, London and New York: Brassey's, 1991, pp.49–50.

3 See C. von Clausewitz, *On War*, ed. M. Howard and P. Paret, Princeton, NJ: Princeton University Press, 1989.

4 I discuss the implications of collapsed states for liberal political thought in my book *Two Faces of Liberalism*, London and

New York: Polity Press and The New Press, 2002, pp.131–3.

5 For an examination of the globalisation of organised crime, see Manuel Castells, *End of Millennium*, London and New York: Blackwells, 1998, Chapter 3.

6 For the most detailed and authoritative study of Al Qaeda to have been published to date, see Rohan Gunaratna's superb book *Inside Al Qaeda, Global Network of Terror*, London: Hurst and Company, 2002.

7 Gunaratna, *Inside Al Qaeda*, p.11.

8 Ibid., p.96.

9 Ibid., p.11.

10 Ruthven, *A Fury for God: The Islamist Attack on America*, London and New York: Granta, 2002, p.199.

11 Ibid., p.197.

12 Gunaratna, *Inside Al Qaeda*, p.23.

13 Ruthven, *A Fury for God*, p.202.

14 Gunaratna, *Inside Al Qaeda*, pp.17–22.

15 Ibid., pp.43, 49.

16 For an illuminating discussion of the role of family networks in Scottish merchant capitalism, see Neal Ascherson, *Stone Voices: The Search for Scotland*, London and New York: Granta, 2002. For the argument that modern capitalism developed from nationalism, see Liah Greenfeld, *The Spirit of Capitalism: Nationalism and Economic Growth*, Cambridge, Mass., and London: Harvard University Press, 2001.

17 The case against the US declaring war after September 11th was made by the British military historian Sir Michael Howard in a lecture, 'September 11 and After: Reflections on the War on Terrorism', at University College, London, on 29 January 2002.

18 For a discussion of the 'revolution in military affairs' see Paul Hirst, *War and Power in the 21st Century*, Cambridge: Polity Press, 2001, pp.88–97.

7 Pax Americana?

1 William Pfaff, *Barbarian Sentiments: How the American*

Century Ends, New York: Hill and Wang, The Noonday Press, 1989, p.5. For an extraordinarily prescient analysis of western political religion, see Edmund Stillman and William Pfaff, *The Politics of Hysteria: The Sources of Twentieth Century Conflict*, London: Victor Gollancz, 1964.

2 For statistics on British overseas investment during the last decades of the nineteenth century, see Niall Ferguson, *The Cash Nexus: Money and Power in the Modern World 1700–2000*, London and New York: Allen Lane/Penguin Press, 2002, p.297 et seq.

3 Ferguson, *The Cash Nexus*, p.312. For a useful overview of the conflict between American hegemonic ambitions and American economic weakness, see Immanuel Wallerstein, 'The Eagle Has Crash Landed', *Foreign Policy*, August/September 2002.

4 For extracts from the paper outlining the new national security strategy of the Bush administration, see the *Financial Times*, 21 September 2002, p.8.

5 For a useful overview of drugs and terrorism, see John Cooley, *Unholy Wars: Afghanistan, America and International Terrorism*, London and Sterling, Virginia, 1999, Chapter 7.

6 Philip Bobbit gives a powerful defence of the theory that market states are replacing nation-states in his book *The Shield of Achilles*, London and New York: Allen Lane/Penguin Press, 2002.

7 I discuss the difficulties of assessing political legitimacy in my book *Two Faces of Liberalism*, London and New York: Polity Press and The New Press, 2002, pp.106–10.

8 For a compelling defence of a new form of the institution of empire, see Robert Cooper, 'The Next Empire', *Prospect*, October 2001. See also Sebastian Mallaby, 'The Reluctant Imperialist: Terrorism, Failed States and the Case for American Empire', *Foreign Affairs*, March/April 2002.

9 George Santayana, *Dominations and Powers: Reflections on Liberty, Society and Government*, Clifton: Augustus M. Kelley, 1972, p.459.

8 Why we still do not know what it means to be modern

1 E. M. Cioran, *History and Utopia*, London: Quartet Books, 1996, p.91.

2 See Samuel Johnson, *The Major Works including Rasselas*, ed. D. Greene, Oxford: Oxford World's Classics, 2002.

3 The quote from Gibbon is cited in John Lukacs, *At the End of an Age*, New Haven and London: Yale University Press, 2002, p.6.

4 Stuart Hampshire, 'Justice is Strife', *Proceedings and Addresses of the American Philosophical Association*, vol. 65, no. 3, November 1991, pp.24–5. See also Hampshire's splendid little book *Justice is Conflict*, Princeton, NJ, and Oxford: Princeton University Press, 2002.

5 Alasdair MacIntyre, *After Virtue: A Study in Moral Theory*, London: Duckworth, 1981, p.85.

6 A. C. Graham, *Disputers of the Tao: Philosophical Argument in Ancient China*, La Salle, Illinois: Open Court, 1989, p.317.

7 Paul Feyerabend, *Conquest of Abundance: A Tale of Abstraction versus the Richness of Being*, Chicago and London: University of Chicago Press, 1999, p.152. For an account of the relations of theoretical knowledge and historical traditions on the development of modern science, see Feyerabend's *Farewell to Reason*, London and New York: Verso, 1987, Chapter 3.

8 L. Wittgenstein, *Tractatus Logico-Philosophicus*, trans. D. F. Pears and B. McGuiness, London and New York: Routledge, 1974, 6.52, p.88.

9 I have discussed the fate of the Tasmanian aboriginal people in *Straw Dogs: Thoughts on Humans and Other Animals*, London and New York: Granta Books, 2002, pp.91–2.

10 I have discussed the ways in which technological globalisation undermines the global free market in *False Dawn: The Delusions of Global Capitalism*, London and New York: Granta Books, 2002, Chapter 3.

11 For a brilliant defence of the pagan virtues in politics and war, see Robert D. Kaplan, *Warrior Politics: Why Leadership*

Demands a Pagan Ethos, New York: Random House, 2002.

12 Edmund Stillman and William Pfaff, *The Politics of Hysteria: The Sources of Twentieth Century Conflict*, London: Victor Gollancz, 1964, p.29.

Index